HAUNTED
OLD TOWN SPRING

Tonya,
Happy Haunting
Your friend from
the [illegible]
Cathy Nance

HAUNTED
OLD TOWN SPRING

CATHY NANCE

Haunted America

Published by Haunted America
A Division of The History Press
Charleston, SC
www.historypress.net

Front cover: author's collection.
Back cover: courtesy Spring Historical Museum; *inset*: courtesy Spring Historical Museum.

First published 2017

Manufactured in the United States

ISBN 9781625859228

Library of Congress Control Number: 2017940947

CONTENTS

Contents

ACKNOWLEDGEMENTS

I would like to say that I have a wonderful support system with family and friends! The first person I would like to thank is my husband, Bill Nance, for all the years of supporting my research in paranormal as well as all of my other endeavors. You allowed me to pursue my ideas no matter how overwhelming it would seem. I know that all of the travel and time that I have invested over the years could not have been done if it weren't for your unending love and support.

My children grew up going in and out of many haunted places with me. I want to thank Taylor Nance for being the first person to put the idea in my head of going out to investigate and then getting all excited to go out with me. We are not just mother and son but also good friends. To both Taylor and Jordan Nance, I say "thank you" for being wide-eyed and inquisitive, putting aside whatever fears you may have had. You came out on investigations that happened to fall on your birthdays—instead of being at a skating rink, we were in the dark somewhere, trying to help someone who was scared and needed our help. There were birthdays in these special places when, after a few hours of investigating, we would turn on the lights, sing happy birthday, blow out candles, eat cake and then turn the lights back off. Because you did this, we have many great memories that most kids don't have. Over the years, Taylor took it upon himself to set up and maintain the equipment. I want to thank my son Paul for being truly an angel on earth, grounding me. I'm not sure what I would be doing in my life without you.

ACKNOWLEDGEMENTS

I want to thank my mother, Patricia Robinson, for telling me that I could do anything or be anyone I wanted in life. You loved me and gave me a strong spiritual foundation through years of private school and religious study; all the years of being overprotective and driving me to school. I always had access to books, unlimited paper and crayons. You encouraged my outside-the-box thinking and creativity with lots of laughs. Thank you for being my friend and for listening to me talk about all the endless ideas that have come out of my head.

I want to acknowledge all the old and new members of my group, Woodlands Paranormal: Bill Nance, Taylor Nance, Jordan Nance, Logan Corelli, Kenneth Melton, Dakota Wesley, Mitch Martino, Mike Bolender, Michael Ferro, Jill Staigerwald Bryan, Dale Zilar, Marleena Mooneyham, Todd Dreher, Bryan Malis, Cathy Malis, Ed Villarreal, Gian Gonzales, Rob Colson, Robeo Umwech, Louis Chebret Jr., Leihia Carol Rogers, Cory Logan, Sasha Frances Landry Hudson, Richard Montes, Laramie Gilbert, Randy Gilbert, Robert E. Bannon and Steve Stark. Thank you for coming out, devoting hours to listen to audio, going through photographs and reviewing videotape. Without all of that effort, we would not have gained the evidence we have. Thank you for helping all of our clients to have peace of mind; we have been able to help so many. They have called us at all hours of the day and night for years, scared and in need of us to come out as soon as we could. They appreciate you, as well.

I need to thank my colleagues for all the years of collaboration in order to help businesses and homeowners with their hauntings. We have learned a great deal from one another and have helped many along the way. Special thanks to: Peter Haviland, Dakota Lawrence, Mike Rickseeker, Chris Borthick, Martha Hazzard Decker, Larry Flaxman, Brad Kling, Joe Stidham, Maria Elena Santos, Father Robert Hall, Jennifer Hanson, Rita Louise, Dash Beardsley, Dee Parks, Patricia Norman, Jennifer Shirley Aills, Jeromy Jones, Christy Clark, Mike McCaskill, Carl Johnson and many others.

Thank you to all of the business and homeowners in Old Town Spring: Rachel Walker O'Neil, Mary Ann Pizzolato, Isabel Cortez Montealvo, Rhonda Lee Schwob, Tammy Williams, Dee Adams, Rachel Stevenson, Jessica Dollinger Lynn, Matthew Lynn, Sharon Richardson, Rowan Dark, Jenny Burroughs Wright, Patricia Rickard, Robert Griffin Dutkiewicz, Darkforest Ivy, Betty Pierce, Heidi Bothmann, Lauren Matney, Shelly Smith, Margaret Mallott Smith, David Mallott, Shirley Clayton, Tommy Phillips, Matthew Potter, Chris and Ginger Pennell, Bryan Melton and Scott,

Kathleen Wilson, Lisa Manske, Maria Gagis Macri and Mandy Holverson, as well as those who wanted to remain anonymous. I enjoyed all of our conversations and meeting you all.

Thank you for your help, spending your time encouraging me and speaking with me about your experiences: Rick Mercer, Teena Richardson, Bill Curd, Jana Beck, Lupe Martinez, Angela Riel, Terri Lofton, Victoria Pettit, Leslie Gutierrez, Charlene Molina, Tiffany Kroschel and Ilyana Peraza.

INTRODUCTION

My husband received an offer to move up in his company with the caveat that we would have to relocate out of state to the area of Spring, Texas. I remember driving through Old Town Spring for the first time while trying to decide if the move would be good for our family. It was dark when we drove through town, and it looked so quaint and like a lovely place to spend time. I believe that one of the reasons I decided to move to Spring was the feeling that Old Town gave me. We moved to Spring in the winter of 2002. After we got unpacked and settled in, I spent time looking in Old Town Spring for a building to house my business. Unfortunately, there were no available buildings at that time. On an off over the years, I would return to look for a business location. I finally found one that suited my needs.

I was always interested in anything related to the paranormal. In 2007, I had an opportunity to join a paranormal group and become one of its investigators. I was soon assigned the job of case manager for the team. I have been all over the United States investigating claims of hauntings since that time. It has been a fun and challenging way of life for me and my family. As a spiritual person, my passion in life has always been to help people, which I have done through my career in nursing, my photography and my other activities. Helping people to know if their "hauntings" were all in their head or real was an easy addition.

I love Old Town Spring. I love the history and the stories of the wonderful people who made this town what it is. At first glance, the title *Haunted Old Town Spring* conjures scary—perhaps evil—connotations, but that is not what

An easy-to-use visual map of Old Town Spring, showing where to start and where to walk to see each store. *Author's illustration.*

Old Town Spring is. It's a place with amazing people and good memories. My goal is to share some of the history and ghost stories with you. Ideally, you can enjoy walking around town with this book as your guide.

I hope you go in and out of the many buildings and others that are not included in my book and see the them from the inside, meet the shop owners and take home some goodies from the town so you will remember being here. I personally love to collect things, especially from locations that have claims of hauntings. I hope Old Town Spring gets under your skin to the point that you want to come back again and again.

OLD TOWN SPRING
403 MAIN STREET
SPRING, TX 77373

The city of Spring is located off Interstate 45, just twenty miles north of Houston in north Harris County. In 2003, it was designated a Texas Historic Landmark. This lovely turn-of-the-century town has an interesting past. The first known inhabitants were the Orcoquiza Indians. They were in turn first visited by Spaniards in 1746. In the 1820s, a number of Austin colonists settled in the area. A trading post was established in 1838 by William

Pierport, a settler from Connecticut. In 1840, Spring had a population of 153. In the 1840s, immigrants from Germany began settling and farming the land. In 1846, land could be purchased for between ten and twenty-five cents per acre.

In 1871, the railroad came through. A group of railroad workers named the area "Camp Spring" following one of the worst winters in Texas history. They were looking forward to better weather. Camp Spring was then platted by the International–Great Northern Railroad Company and became a permanent settlement. The word "Camp" was dropped, and Spring became the official name of the town. It was the base of operations for the workers and became a boomtown as a result of all the business the railroad brought in. By 1878, there were enough residents for a post office to be established. Spring became a crossroads for two intersecting rail lines in 1901. The yard then added a roundhouse and fourteen track yards. The railroad had almost two hundred workers living here at the time. Residents grew their own sugar cane and brought it to the local mill, which was located to the right side as one entered Old Town Spring at the split in the road. During the years of growth, Spring had not only a sugar mill for syrup manufacturing but

Spring Depot, photograph taken in 1900 from a postcard. *Courtesy Spring Historical Museum.*

also two cotton gins, five saloons, an opera house, a hospital, two steam sawmills, a gristmill, a bank, hotels, three churches, several schools and even a gambling hall. The town comprised about twelve hundred people by 1910.

The decline came in 1915, when a storm made landfall on the Texas coast as a Category 4 hurricane with sustained winds of 135 miles per hour. It had a devastating effect on Spring, damaging the opera house on Spring School Road and destroying the train depot. The railroad headquarters moved to Houston in 1923. Prohibition and the Great Depression forced many businesses to close. The town was reduced to a small settlement. Russel Day Lily Farm helped the economy through those tough years. People of the town would entertain themselves with movies or dancing at the Woodsman of the World Hall on Aldine Westfield Road. The nearby opera house showed early movies.

In the late 1960s, business-minded individuals started to return to Old Town Spring, turning their homes into shops. The Goodyear airship *America* was based in Spring from 1969 through 1992, when it was moved to Akron, Ohio. The oil boom that began in the 1970s helped make the town grow and become what it is today. In 1980, the Old Town Spring Association was formed to promote the area as a shopping destination. By 1989, Old Town Spring had become a tourist attraction, with many unique specialty shops. Museums, art galleries and restaurants are within an easy stroll from one another. People from all over the world have come to visit. The town has several annual festivals and events, including the Texas Crawfish & Music Festival, which draws approximately fifty thousand visitors. The town is also voted one of the top attractions in Texas each year.

Old Town Spring is affectionately known as the most haunted town in Texas. Television personality Debra Duncan dubbed Old Town Spring "The Ghost Capital of Texas" in one of her stories. Paranormal groups and television crews have visited to catch evidence of the reported activity. The many stories of spirits bring in people from all over looking to have their own experience with a ghost. At this time, scientifically, nobody knows why there are so many sightings of ghosts and other paranormal activity. Perhaps we will discover the reason someday.

PART I

A WALKING TOUR OF HAUNTED OLD TOWN SPRING

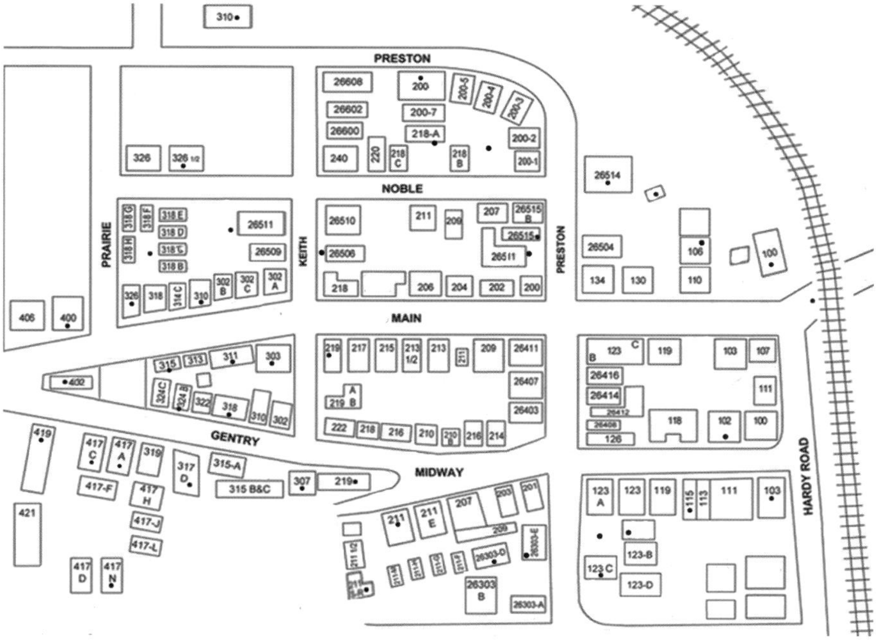

Map of Old Town Spring showing the buildings along with their addresses, to make it easy to find each site. *Author's illustration.*

Spring Historical Museum

403 Main Street
Spring, TX 77373

In front of the building there is a path with a sitting area around a fountain. A historical marker, placed there on July 18, 2004, states:

> *Initially a farming community supported by sugar cane and cotton crops, Spring was platted by the Houston & Great Northern Railroad in 1873. That same year, Callahan Pickette became the town's first postmaster. Spring served as the commercial center for the surrounding area during the early 1900s and a focal point for German settlers including Carl Wunsche, who was instrumental in the town's development. A new rail line reached Spring in the early 20th century, and the addition of a roundhouse and railway shops created an import rail center for the growing community. Developer R.I. Robinson subdivided land south of the original town and the commercial area shifted to accommodate the rail junction. Railroads facilitated the development of the lumber industry, which boasted a number of mills, both large and small, in the boom era of lumber production. With the boom came the need for new businesses including hotels, saloons, an opera house, gambling houses, a hospital, and a bank. In 1907, residents established the Spring Independent School District. The loss of the roundhouse and the onset of Prohibition led to a decline in population. Ultimately, the saloons, hotels, and other rail-supported businesses closed*

Left: The historic marker in front of the museum. *Author's collection.*

Below: The Spring Historical Museum, which occupies a former courthouse, is located at 403 Main Street. Several spirits are said to be in the building, including a couple that loves to dance to music coming from the woman's Victrola. *Author's collection.*

in the 1920s. The dwindling community persisted, however, creating a volunteer fire department in the 1950s and sustaining the Spring ISD, which integrated in the mid-1960s. As the population began to grow again in the early 1970s, new businesses opened including many specialty shops. Spring continues to attract new residents and businesses, but retains its unique identity as a town with a strong German heritage and its link to early history.

This building was constructed in the 1940s as the Spring Church of Christ. Harris County acquired and remodeled it to serve as the courthouse. It housed the offices of the constable, deputy sheriff and highway patrol for many years. It was designated as a Texas Historical Landmark in 2003.

Today, it serves as the Spring Historical Museum, housing artifacts from Spring's past. One of those items is a hand-cranked 1900-era Victrola previously belonging to Marie Bailey. It is said that, mysteriously, it plays a song reportedly favored by the original owner. Bailey brought it when she traveled from St. Louis to be with a man named Albert Faetzhold, whom her father forbade her from seeing. They were wed despite her father's objections and lived their lives in Spring, where they were devoted to each other until their deaths in the 1970s. They loved spending nights listening to music and dancing.

Today, it is said that you can see a young couple dancing in each other's arms to the music on nights of full moons. The woman wears what looks like a lacy bridal gown. It is believed to be the couple just described. It has also been reported that, on several occasions, without explanation, the Victrola would start by itself and play. Sometimes, the music is heard right after the lights go off and the museum closes. Some members of the historical society say they have heard music or noises resembling the Victrola playing.

Sometimes, an object is so loved by the person who owned it that their energy gets imprinted or recorded on it. That kind of haunting is what is called a residual haunting. It's like a recording playing over and over when the conditions are right. Science doesn't yet understand what conditions are most favorable for this phenomenon.

In a residual haunting, the energy is somehow recorded—the mechanism of how it gets recorded or imprinted is not known. The recordings can be captured and imprinted on stone, as on old wood, slate or other materials, like iron nails or crystal quarts and many times have an underground water source. There is an unknown environmental condition that happens to record the event. We also don't know exactly the mechanism or sequence of

The Victrola in the museum, which houses the spirits of a couple whose love is so strong that they still dance by the light of the moon. *Author's collection.*

events that will allow it to be replayed. Perhaps a heightened emotional state of a living person, high humidity or barometric pressure play a part; again, we don't know. If we did understand it, we would create that condition over and over again and study it in-depth to understand it. We do see some patterns. For example, a haunting is usually of an emotional nature—traumatic or violent.

When the playback of the event happens, energy is dispersed. The haunting is really a playback of an event that took place in the same spot. The haunting will happen often, at the same time of day, and the spirit does not interact with any person or the environment. The apparitions you may see are not intelligent spirits but recordings of the event.

When the playback of the event happens, energy is dispersed, and this can make doors open or shut, create noises or produce ghostly apparitions. Many famous hauntings are residual and not what we call intelligent. The most famous is the Brown Lady of Raynham Hall, photographed by Captain Hubert Provand and his assistant Indre Shira while they were taking pictures of the historic Raynham Hall for *Country Life* magazine in the late afternoon of September 19, 1936. The photo was the first known capture of a spirit. Lady Dorothy Walpole is the person thought to be the Brown Lady. She still walks the staircase, looking for her five children. Walpole was born in 1686 and "officially" died of smallpox in 1726.

Her tragic story began after her father refused to grant his consent for her to marry her first love, Charles Townshend, Second Viscount Townshend. Dorothy was married off to someone else then began an affair with Townshend. When her husband found out, he ordered that she be kept locked in her apartments at Raynham Hall. As further punishment, he prohibited her children from being around her. Unofficially, she died the age of forty of either a broken heart or a broken neck after being pushed down the grand staircase.

Another example of a residual haunting is the Treasurer's Grand House in York, England, which dates from the seventeenth or eighteenth century. This is the example I use most frequently to explain a residual haunting to clients. The city of York has stood since A.D. 71, when the Roman Ninth Legion built a fortress with six thousand soldiers. The house stands within the area of the old Roman barracks. The Minster Treasurers lived in this house until the Reformation. The last treasurer was William Cliff in 1547. The title was discontinued because there was no longer a need for a treasurer. The area of the house where residual hauntings can be witnessed is in the cellar. There, when conditions are right, Roman soldiers march two by two through the wall and into the opposite wall. These soldiers never interact with anyone; they only march where you can see it and hear it. Apparently, over the years, the soldiers' legs have gotten shorter, to the point that it looks like they are waking on their knees. You may be wondering why they would be on their knees. One day, the cellar was excavated, and the Roman road was found two feet beneath the floor.

The Tower of London's ghost of Queen Anne Boleyn is another great example. Anne could not bear a son for her husband, Henry VIII. He became convinced that their marriage was cursed. He had his eye on Jane

The bench inside the former courthouse. *Author's collection.*

Delivery wagon for Goedecke, seen in a photograph taken in 1899. *Courtesy Spring Historical Museum.*

Seymour, who eventually became his wife. She gave him a son, Edward VI (1537–1553). In order to get rid of Anne, Henry falsely accused her of treason, witchcraft, adultery and even incest with her brother. Five men accused of being with Anne eventually confessed under torture and were executed on Tower Hill on May 17, 1536. Anne was executed two days later. This emotional and violent series of events led to the residual haunting.

The guards, known as the "Yeomen of the Guard," have watched the tower since 1509. They have many stories of seeing the ghost of Anne. One guard reported watching Anne lead a courtly procession across the tower green and toward Tower Hill, where she had been executed. In another story, a group of guards saw her appear so close that one of them was able to poke into the apparition before it faded in front of them.

Sometimes, a house will be remodeled, but the activity of a residual haunting will remain. The spirit will walk through what was a door but is now a wall. It will climb stairs that were once there but have long since been removed, perhaps as a result of a fire. This activity continues to occur under the right conditions and usually at the same time of day. If the staircase in Raynham Hall is ever demolished, I am sure that, under the right conditions, people will continue to see the Brown Lady—this time, floating down on what would have been the stairs.

I hope you now have a better understanding of what a residual haunting is and know that there is no reason for anyone to be afraid of such residual activity. It is an amazing event that allows people to witness the past—much like watching a movie. The Spring Historical Museum houses many things from the past that could contain some amount of residual energy.

THE DOLL HOSPITAL

419 Gentry Street #102
Spring, TX 77373

The building housing the Doll Hspital is not original to Old Town Spring. Mary Ann Pizzolato, the owner of the doll hospital, tells me that nothing out of the ordinary has happened to her while she has been here. She does restoration and repair of old dolls. She believes that no doll is too old or too new to have work done. According to an article on the doll hospital's website taken from the *Dallas Morning News*, "Thousands of cracked, unstrung and disrobed dolls have sipped from the fountain of youth. The oldest ones date from the mid-1700s, when they were shaped by hand from sticky wax. There are 1950s bobby sox figures [and] Depression-era Shirley Temple dolls."

All of these beautiful dolls, many with long histories, are just waiting for a new home. But some people are afraid of dolls. Parapsychologist Peter James Haviland Acch of Lone Star Spirits talked to me about something in his field called "place memory," in which our psychic selves pick up on an event that is attached to an object. This could be all the love and happiness someone had while carrying a doll around, now a residual place memory. Someone can pick up an item like an old doll and feel happy. Many times, though, place memory is associated with a traumatic event. A person who fears dolls may want to avoid the doll hospital—all these dolls in one place. Most of the memories associated with the dolls are good, but perhaps some bad memories exist, as well.

The Doll Hospital is located at 419 Gentry Street. One night, Kingwood Paranormal was conducting a ghost box session and audio recorders on the porch. They collected several intelligent responses to questions from spirits. What could be here? *Author's collection.*

I have had a few people tell me they investigated around the building and became scared and ran off. Old Town Spring has many such stories, but there are none about this particular store or any its dolls. Perhaps it was an irrational fear of dolls that made them think of investigating here. This fear is known as pediophobia. Paranormal investigator Tyler Brown has this fear of dolls. In 2014, his organization, Kingwood Paranormal Group (KPG), uploaded a video to YouTube of an investigation they did. They were running a ghost box session outside of the doll hospital, specifically because one of their members was deathly afraid of dolls.

A ghost box, also known as "Frank's box," is a useful tool in the investigation of the paranormal. The device is used to communicate with the spirit world. Ghost boxes are modified radios that constantly scan the airwaves, sweeping and bypassing channels instead of stopping on a specific station. It plays each one for a fraction of a second. My favorite time to listen is when there is more static, which is called "white noise," rather than slowly scanning the radio, when you really can discern the radio stations. The idea is that spirits can come through on whatever unknown frequency there is by which to communicate. We record these sessions with an audio recorder for later review. Sometimes, voices can be heard. The voices can respond to questions we ask. Over the years, we have had some interesting results with these sessions.

On the night of KPG's investigation, the members got multiple responses on the ghost box. (The results can be heard by searching the Internet for "Old Town Spring doll hospital" or "Kingwood Paranormal Group.") After turning on the ghost box, they asked the spirits, "Can you tell me how old you are?" They received responses of "five," "eight" and "eight." They next asked, "Do you like dolls?" and got the response "Gay, yes." They asked a couple more questions and then heard "Don't" when they asked if they could move one of the dolls. Tyler then asked if there were any evil dolls in the building. The response sounded like "You betcha." It was asked again if they could move one of the dolls. "Yes" was the response and, later, what sounded like "Tyler." Toward the end of the video, Tyler tells the spirits that he is going to shut the session down. What sounds like "Hold on" is then heard. These responses seem to be from something intelligent.

Intelligent responses seem to point to a possible haunting. There are stories from around the world of hauntings associated with items such as

Inside the Doll Hospital, where you can find dolls from as early as the 1700s. *Photo courtesy of Mary Ann Pizzolato.*

dolls, perhaps from voodoo rituals. One of the most famous instances is that of Robert the Doll, which was donated to the Key West Art and Historical Society. He is in a case in the Fort East Martello Museum and Gardens. This creepy-looking doll, four feet tall, is made from rags and stuffed with straw. It even has hair stitched on its head. It was given as a present in 1906 to a boy named Robert Eugene Otto by his former caretaker several days after they fired her. Soon after he received the present, Robert stopped using his first name. He told his parents that the doll wanted to be called Robert. This doll inspired the movie *Child's Play* and its character Chucky. It was reported by numerous sources that Robert the doll would move from one window to the next, talk, change facial expressions and move. Items were reported to be moved or broken. It was eventually put away in the attic by the boy's parents. Eugene Otto grew up, became a famous artist in Key West and eventually got married. His parents passed away, and the doll finally came out of the attic to spend its days with Eugene until 1974. It was then locked in a trunk and later found by new residents of the house. It terrified the couple's ten-year-old daughter and was then donated to the Key West Art and Historical Society.

Today, people come to see the famous doll and are warned about taking pictures—unless Robert gives his permission by tilting his head or by following a strict protocol. First, you must introduce yourself; second, take the photograph; finally, thank Robert when you're done, or else bad things will happen. People from all over the world have written to Robert, including a letter from America's forty-third president, George W. Bush. Most of the letters involve people begging the doll for forgiveness for taking its picture without permission. Museum employees tell of finding the doll in various locations around the museum. One worker says that the doll attacked him one evening during a thunderstorm. The man, who was then in his seventies, said he never returned to the museum. He told one of the paranormal investigation groups that he was sitting at his desk one night when he saw the doll run across the room and hop up on the end of the desk where he was sitting. According to the man, the doll was very much alive, giggling a weird laugh and telling him that he would die that night. One of his coworkers said that, the next morning, Robert was found lying on the floor of the museum.

There are no stories of hauntings of any of the dolls that have come through the doll hospital here in Spring. This is a unique place to visit and spend time looking at all the dolls, some of which are older and historical. Imagine owning a doll from the mid-1700s. All of the dolls need places to live and need your consideration in taking one home.

Resting in the World

417 Gentry Street
Spring, TX 77373

This building was moved from another location to help bring more space to Old Town Spring. The shop Resting in the World now occupies the space. Isabel Cortez Montealvo used to lease the building for her bakery, the Cake Faery. She talked about the spirit of a man who she believed occupied her shop and would shove her customers around and do other things. She told me:

> *I moved into the building I want to say about March 2011, but I'm not sure I was there two months before the Crawfish Festival. I noticed him the first time I went to the Cake Faery alone when we were getting the place ready for the grand opening. He was visible to me in my mind's eye. He was an older gentleman in his mid-sixties, tall, heavy-set; not fat but stocky. If that makes sense. I don't think he was aware he had crossed over. I could feel something pushing me back, not wanting to let me in. Sometimes a shove. Once I got in, I confronted him and told him he was not going to make me leave. That if we couldn't live in peace I would bring everything I knew and would push him out! So we lived in peace and became friendly after that. Once we learned to get along after a while, he was protective of me. On my closed days I would schedule pickups. Customers would tell me when the spirit would be peeking in, that they could feel someone shove*

them away, that someone was watching them and made them feel like they shouldn't go in. His favorite time of the year was Christmas. He would go around humming; lol he loves that season.

This type of activity sounds like what we call an intelligent haunting. Residual hauntings do not push people around or interact with them. An intelligent haunting resembles a real person who is trying to get you to notice them—but you cannot see them. The activity they create occurs at different times of the day and has no discernible pattern of occurrence. They can move about the environment freely and even move from one location to another. For whatever reason, intelligent hauntings can happen within a small area. It's as if they are attached by an invisible chain or rope to a spot. That spot can be associated with an object, person or place. The activity can be nice, like the smell of your grandpa's cologne, or bad. But for most of the living, the activity is scary either way.

The man who is here could have been attached to the land or, more likely, came in with the house that was moved here. I do not have any further history on the house. Isabel told me that she knew what he looked like, so she asked psychics to come in and investigate the building and tell her what they got from her property. She wanted to know everything they saw and felt. She told me, "I did not give them any info that I knew other than a spirit was there. They described him to me to a T. He was even aggressive with one to the point that I had to calm him down. One of the psychics left because she felt attached to him and couldn't handle it, but as I said he had become protective of me."

Isabel seems to have abilities in the psychic realm; most people do without even realizing it. During her interview, she was concerned that I not look at her like she was crazy. Many people feel exactly the way she does regarding not only any kind of psychic ability but any kind of paranormal activity that has happened to them. The first thing people say to me when they call is, "Please don't think I'm crazy, but…." Isabel said this about her abilities:

I don't call myself a physic. I never have, but I have always been very perceptive and a good judge of character. I sometimes know ahead of time things that will happen or that will come to pass. I have always been able to interpret dreams. I can do other things too, naturally, and I always have, so it has just been a part of me. I never considered that I was physic, but I have to deal with the fact I was raised in the church and that it was frowned upon. So, I always hid what I have sensed. Today I just say my "Spidey" senses are going off.

Next to Resting in the World is the former space owned by Shelly Smith, who owns Different Strokes Pet Boutique, which used to be located next door in unit D. She also has stories of hearing people talk and go up and down stairs in her old space but finding nobody there. She also has some pictures she can show you. She told me, "We had two kids' spirits that were there most of the time—Ralph and Polly."

Another of the stories about the general area of town behind the shop took place many years ago. There was an accident with one of the many traveling carnivals. A child and a man were riding on a Ferris wheel. A malfunction of some type took place, and the child fell to the ground and died, most likely from head trauma. Many people report seeing a child that looks like a little boy who seems to be lost or looking for someone. When they go to approach him to help, he disappears without a trace. I have heard "Poof, he is gone," and people say their mind starts spinning. They think all kinds of things: they were just seeing things, or their mind was playing tricks on them. Some also report seeing a man. Psychics have said that they believe these two souls are looking for each other. The man is probably the boy's father or grandfather. The little boy doesn't seem to know or understand that he passed away; he thinks he is lost.

The Blue Giraffe

417 Gentry Street
Spring, TX 77373

The D. Kaplan Feed Store and Dry Goods opened in a wood house at 2200 Yale in 1913. The Heights at that time was considered a distant suburb of Houston. The store, owned and operated by David Kaplan and his wife, Bessie, was located on the first floor, and the family lived on the second floor with their two sons, Bennett and Herman.

They renamed the store in the beginning of the 1920s Kaplan's and then moved across the street to 2125 Yale. Kaplan's expanded into a brick department store and added a brick extension that they named Ben-Hur, which reflected the brothers' names. The stores finally moved into Kaplan's Ben-Hur in the 1950s and then expanded. Martin, Bennet's son, joined the business in 1975 and took over running the business in 1981 when his father passed away. In 2005, when Martin was sixty years old, he finally decided to close the store after years of declining sales. The two-acre property was put up for sale.

The original D. Kaplan Feed Store and Dry Goods building in the Heights was taken apart in two sections and relocated to its current location at 417 Gentry in Old Town Spring. It seems that the essence of Martin Kaplan has moved along with the building. He had prided himself on personal contact with his customers and maintaining those relationships. The current owner is exactly the same way.

The Blue Giraffe and Kudos are located at 417 Gentry Street. Both buildings are more than one hundred years old and were moved to Old Town Spring from the Heights. Both are also actively haunted by spirits. *Author's collection.*

Now known as the Blue Giraffe, it opened on February 24, 2015, as a coffee shop serving, food, beer, wine and all of the assorted coffee drinks. It features an open mic night every Thursday. The establishment is family owned and operated. I was told by the owner, Rhonda Lee Schwob, that the building is haunted. The shade of a lamp upstairs would come on and off on its own, freaking out anyone who saw it. No matter how many times the shade would be put on, it would be taken off again soon thereafter. A stuffed rabbit belonging to the store was once found outside near a tree stump for no reason. The family members had no idea who put it there. It somehow came out of storage on its own. Another interesting part of this story is that it occurred around Easter. Tammy, who owns Kudos, next door to the Blue Giraffe, told Rhonda that the former owner of the building, when it used to be Home Sweet Home, would set a rabbit on that same tree stump. Maybe the spirit that lives in this building needs everything to stay the way it used to be. As they say, old habits die hard.

KUDOS

417A Gentry Street
Spring, TX 77373

Today, Kudos is a collection of small shops brought together in one store. There are unique, beautifully handcrafted treasures as well as collectibles of all kinds. This building, brought from the Heights many years ago, is more than 105 years old. You can't tell how they took it apart to move it by looking at it from the outside. Tammy Williams, the owner of Kudos, has talked with me several times about her experiences in the store:

> *I was really not a big believer and all that, but living that* [haunting] *has convinced me that it's real. There were people coming into the store and telling me it was haunted. We were like, "Yeah, right." One day, my husband went up to take a nap upstairs—we have a twin bed up there—and while he was asleep, that bed lifted up into the air and it came down, bam!, like that. Since then, my husband has a thing where he won't go back upstairs. About a week later, we had this lady come into the store. We were having a few odd things happening. You know, we have a toy corner in the store where we have toys. I would come in, and there would be toys all on the floor in front of the building, but that corner is in the back. I would say to my employees, "Why don't you start picking this stuff up?," you know, and they would tell me, "We didn't do it." About a week after that happened with my husband*

> *with the bed, a psychic lady came by and told me that there were children in that house along with a man, and there was a little boy saying that he was very sorry but he would put the toys back the next time. Then she said, "Oh, they're laughing right now, they said they are sorry that they scared the man in the bed." I was so scared I almost wet my pants. We had not told anybody this information. How would she know that?*

Another lady kept telling Tammy that she needed to put lace upstairs because lace means that you are welcoming something and that you mean them no harm. She told me about a scary thing that happened to her one late night. One day, a lady came into the store and told her that their family had once owned the building when it was a feed store. They lived upstairs, and the feed store was downstairs with a grocery store. They told Tammy that they had two children who had died of tuberculosis in the 1920s or the '30s. It had coincided with everything that had happened, which just further enhanced Tammy's belief in the paranormal. Tammy said, "I went to the bathroom one day only after I locked the front to the store, then went to the bathroom. I heard what sounded like someone whistling. I thought it had to be a radio. When I came out, there was no radio, and nobody in the store. You can hear footsteps upstairs and nobody ever bothers us, though. You can hear footsteps walking while we are all downstairs. They come down the stairs, too. I'm not afraid anymore, but I know that there is something there."

Tammy also told me about mannequins that she had in the store. Her daughter used to love to play with the dolls' hair, fixing them all up. One day, after she had spent a lot of time working on the dolls, the hair suddenly became messed up. They went back into the store the next day and found all the dolls' hair completely ruined and all over the place. Tammy said that too many weird things happen in this place. You can't be in there at night, but the spirits aren't aggressive. Tammy is used to them now, after years of being around them and hearing them. Some employees of her shop won't work in the evening because they are afraid.

More than one psychic went upstairs with Tammy to check out the building. They told her about seeing the spirits standing in the hallway. One psychic even told Tammy she had just walked through them but she didn't know it. Rowan from After Tours takes her group here to check out the doll in the window that seems to change expressions. She was standing outside Kudos, talking about one night when she took a series of photos when it looked like the doll was shape-shifting. She caught one photo that looks normal. Her next photo showed the doll's mouth slightly open. In the last photo, you can see what looks like a tooth.

About four years ago, a manager was on duty at night in the big barn building behind Kudos. He would see a light like a candle in the one of the upstairs rooms. He spoke of seeing something through the upstairs window. He thought that it looked like a farmer with a straw hat. He also saw what he thought was that same person walking around town. He tried to catch up with it to ask questions, but it disappeared.

Cathy Nance Studios

324 Gentry Street
Spring TX 77373

This small photography studio is where I used to do my portrait work, as well as headshots and glamour and boudoir work. I have since moved into the blue building at 218 Noble Street, which is also haunted. I create fine art that is sold in a few galleries. I also do editorial work for magazines; some of this work I was able to do in this small space. This is not an original building in Old Town Spring; it just may be the tiniest of them all, only nine feet by twenty feet. I had been able to make it work for my business, and I used to run a paranormal group called Woodlands Paranormal from here. When I moved into the building, I did not notice any activity. There is a sense of calm that I get when I'm working in here. I decorated the inside to make it cute and comfortable. I did get a sense of the past here, of the various businesses that have been in the building before me. When I would leave to go home, I would make sure the lights were off, air was set at a decent temperature and things were put up. When I returned, things would be different. I would find my air-conditioning turned off and set at a higher or lower number than what I had it at. Sometimes, lights were on or things were moved. I thought that it was my landlord doing this because of an incident that had happened.

One time not long after I moved into my building, one of my clients told me that they had been in my shop the day before, when it was closed

Cathy Nance Studios at 324 Gentry Street is the previous home of not only my photography studio but also Woodlands Paranormal. It is a place where ancient haunted African artifacts were housed. My collection of haunted artifacts lived here from years of investigating the paranormal. *Author's collection.*

and I was not there. I asked her how that was possible, and she told me that a man was in my building with the door wide open, working on what looked like the electricity. The woman took a tour around the inside of my business. I didn't know anyone was going to be inside my building. From that point on, all strange activity that ever happened was blamed on what I thought was my landlord or a worker coming in. It wasn't until I started talking to other business owners that I found out that quite a few of them had the same type of things happening. Some shop owners told me that they checked every time with their landlords following a strange event and were told that nobody was in the building and that they would never come in without notice, anyway. The building directly behind the studio is the scene of exactly the same activity that I have in mine; the proprietor has also seen a child. I have not noticed anything that would be considered intelligent or negative at all in or around my building, and the vibe of the place is sweet and comforting.

I was told that African artifacts and spiritual items were sold in my building not long before I took over. I think that is interesting because I, too, collect objects and artifacts—but mine are reported to be haunted before I acquire them. Some of these items are stored in my building. For example, I was given a bowling ball with "Earl" engraved above the holes. While teaching a cake-decorating class, one of my students was talking about something weird happening related to this ball. She told me that she was talking to a neighbor in her living room when, all of a sudden, the ball came rolling slowly down the hallway. It rolled up to her and stopped, then it continued rolling and stopped at the neighbor. They we just staring at the ball, trying to figure out what was going on, when it started to roll away from them. My student said, "Oh hell no," and picked up the ball and put it outside. She continued to have weird things happen in the home, like lights turning on or off and things moving around. She buried the ball in the yard. Her dog dug it up a few days later, so she put it in a crevice in a large tree in her yard so that it wouldn't move. She would decorate the ball for holidays and talk to the ball. She believed that sometimes the ball would make bad things happen in her home.

I asked her if she thought her home was haunted, or if the ball was, and she said she didn't know. She told me that I could have the ball because she didn't want it. I was glad to hear that and made arrangements to get the ball. I was going to see if it was the ball or her house that was haunted. I picked up the ball and kept it in the car until I could make time to watch it. It was winter, and I was surprised to find large, weird-looking red ants taking up residence in the holes of the ball. They had come alive in the heat of the car. I brought the ball into my house and watched it to see what would happen. It was like watching paint dry. I have had weird stuff happen, but none that I would definitely say came from the ball.

Another object that made its way to me was a haunted clock. I had heard stories of teams of people investigating the clock and the activity that took place around it. There was even a documentary about this clock, *Dead Time—South Oklahoma City Residence*, made by Logan Corelli. When I was given the opportunity to get the clock, I jumped at the offer. How exciting! I live in Houston, Texas, so my mother, who lives in Oklahoma, had to drive to pick it up for me off of the porch of the house, which is now empty. The owners did not want to take the clock to their new home and, in their minds, infecting their new home with what they thought was evil attached to the clock. They had come into possession of the clock when they moved into a new home and found it in the attic. They brought it down, polished it up, put it on the mantel and wound it up. They believe that the clock comes alive when it is wound up. They had so many stories of things that happened because of the clock.

I listened to parapsychologist Logan Corelli, who investigated the clock. He told me that he took the clock home to test whether it was the house or the clock that had activity. He assured me it was the clock. Logan said that he only had the clock three days and immediately took it back to the homeowner. He told me about large orange spiders resembling tarantulas and a large dog that looked like a wolf, which ran at Logan's car on the way home from picking up the clock, hitting the side of the car before disappearing. I will let Logan tell you his story in his own words:

The first time that I learned anything about the clock is when I went to the residence to investigate a haunting. The homeowners told me about the clock they had found in the attic and felt that the clock was directly related to abusive physical attacks that had occurred to some homeowners and was directly related to the other activity in the house. I had asked permission to take the clock home with me for further research. The homeowners agreed, and we packed the clock in the back of the SUV. On our way home, I looked off into the distance and I saw a long, slender dog-like figure running towards the street we were on. I watched the figure as it met up with the SUV, and its head collided with the door next to me. I looked back and saw the figure shake its head and run across the street into the trees, where it disappeared.

I got home that night and I put the clock on my dresser. I went into the bathroom of my bedroom to prepare for bed. The door to the bathroom was cracked open slightly, and I distinctly heard what sounded like someone walking around inside my bedroom. I opened the door, and nobody was there. The next day, I came home for lunch to get on the computer. As I was sitting at my desk, I heard a noise come from the direction of the clock. It sounded like a tapping or clicking noise—hard to describe it. I called out to the clock directly; when I did, the doorknob to my bedroom door started shaking and was locked. I got my gun and went through the house to see if someone had broken into my house. All doors and windows were locked, and nobody was in the house. Later that night, as I was in the bathroom, the glass door to the clock, which was latched, unexplainably opened on its own. I decided that I was going to wind the clock before I went to bed to see if it would have an effect on anything that could happen. I had gone to bed and fell asleep around 1:30 a.m. and awoke suddenly at 2:30 a.m. When I woke up I saw that there were orange spiders all over the room, including on the blankets on the bed. I immediately flung out of bed, started shaking off, making sure there was nothing on me, no spiders. As soon as I did, I looked at the clock, and it made an ominous mechanical sound as if it was laughing at me. It was at that moment I decided to return the clock to its rightful owners.

Logan believes that it is possible he had a spiritual conflict of interest in bringing the clock inside his house because he already had much activity. There were multiple spirits in his house because he was bringing them home, as well as various transient entities. He had multiple artifacts with attachments, including a possessed monster truck. I now have the clock. It is not running at the moment because I do not want to escalate any activity I could have in my home or business. There are times when I have wound it up and sat with anticipation of activity, but there wasn't any. I can say I was disappointed but haven't really had time to put it to a really good test. I am always skeptical and logical; at this time, it is a clock with an interesting history that has potential.

One night, my group, Woodlands Paranormal, conducted an investigation in the studio and got audio responses from several spirits. We had Bill Curd with us, who is a psychic. He was conducting a back-and-forth conversation using a new audio experiment that Mitch Martino had set up. The different meters we use to investigate were going off all night, as well.

BROOKWOOD COMMUNITY CENTER

318 Gentry Street
Spring, TX 77373

The journey of Brookwood began in 1957, when founder Yvonne Streit's one-year-old daughter, Vicki, became seriously disabled from mumps and encephalitis. As a teacher, Yvonne sought answers to try to heal her daughter and make her life better. She traveled all over the world to get answers on how to educate and enhance her daughter's life. She decided to help more than just her daughter, though. There are 36.2 million functioning disabled adults in the United States. About 8 million of those disabled people need full or partial care for life. Yvonne started Brookwood to try to meet this tremendous need. The community is located in Brookshire, Texas, forty miles west of downtown Houston. It is a nonprofit 501(c)3 residential facility and vocational program for adults with disabilities. It has a few stores outside of Brookshire, including one in Old Town Spring. Among the many buildings on its campus are eight group homes and forty-seven greenhouses serving 110 resident adults. Another 80-plus adults participate in its day program. Brookwood's website states: "Through the Grace of God, The Brookwood Community provides an educational environment that creates meaningful jobs, builds a sense of belonging, and provides meaning and purpose for adults with disabilities."

The store in Old Town Spring is now closed, but it thrived for many years. You would walk through the gate and feel a sense of peace overcome you.

Brookwood Community Store is located at 318 Gentry Street. Mysterious lights are seen through the windows at times and are even caught on surveillance footage from area stores. Some think that angels hover near the disabled people whom this place once served. *Author's collection.*

This was true even for those unaware of the background of the shop. When I moved into my studio a few doors down, the owner of a coffee shop came over to tell me that her security cameras were catching lights moving around, blinking and turning on and off inside the store across the street from her. This store was Brookwood Community Center. She told me that the lights were not orbs, but actual lights, some of them flickering. One night, she went across the street to see if the store was being broken in to, but it appeared that nobody was there, and she no longer saw the lights. Perhaps the lights she kept seeing on her security footage were the angels that surround these members of our community.

We have investigated multiple cases in which light anomalies were a part of the case. Once, we watched what looked like a sparkler going off in the room of a child who had been talking to something or someone unseen. The parents couldn't see anything, and their daughter was too young to talk about it. They were so scared that they called us to come and help them figure it out. We came to believe through the course of the investigation that it could be an angel.

Orbs, as some people call them when they happen to appear in a photograph, are only interesting to paranormal investigators if they can see them with the naked eye or if they emit their own light. It is similar to looking straight into a flashlight or another source of light in the distance, and it can be moving around. Photographs containing orbs that appear to be self-illuminated may actually represent spiritual phenomena at work. In many cases, though, orbs that are captured in photographs are caused simply by particulates floating in the air—dust or beads of moisture that reflect light when they are caught within six inches of the camera. At the moment, we do not have computers that can detect the difference between a dust particle that shows up as an orb and an actual spirit manifesting as an orb. Our paranormal team keeps all the photos we take, including those that show orbs that are most likely dust. We don't put images of orbs on our website and claim they are paranormal. We do show balls of light that appear self-illuminated or streaks of light that appear to be moving.

Envy Wine Room (Chakra Shop and Tarot)

317 Gentry Street #D3
Spring, TX 77373

Located in the front part of the building, Envy Wine Room has unique wine-tasting opportunities. The boutique and gift shop treats its customers to the ultimate sip-and-shop experience. It offers wines and beers from around the world by the glass or by the bottle in a cozy lounge. A Christian woman used to occupy the building that today houses Envy. She started a prayer group that met in her building because she told someone there was too much ghostly activity going on in her building. She would play Christian music all day and even overnight after closing because she believed there was some type of portal that was open, allowing things to cross over. There was too much negativity; she eventually moved to get away.

At the end of Envy Wine Room's building is a shop that used to be the Chakra Shop and Tarot before it moved to 100 Main Street in May 2016. It is now being used as an event area for Envy Wine Room. When Dee Adams and Rachel Stevenson from Chakra Shop and Tarot moved into the building, they started getting unusual help from a female spirit that would bring Dee customers.

Dee and Rachel were originally going to rent a different unit in the big, two-story building. The unit sat to the left, next to the restroom in Gentry Square. They had contractors come out to try to get it ready so the shop could get set up. One night, very late, they didn't have electricity turned on, but enough ambient light was coming through the door for Dee and Rachel to show the contractor what they wanted him to do. All three of them got really scared because something was picked up and thrown across the room, making a loud noise. The contractor got out of there fast. At the crawfish festival about two years ago, a lady came up to Dee and Rachel and asked if they owned any shops here and if they knew anything about the main building on Gentry? Dee told them that before it was moved to Old Town Spring, it had been a boys' home. The woman wanted to go inside and see what it was like now. This made sense to Dee because a lot of the activity in that building was related to what children would do, like the sound of ball-playing and door handles jiggling when you were in the restroom but nobody else was around.

Dee and Rachel were having so much difficulty trying to open the store when Dee noticed the corner unit lit up really brightly, even glowing. She decided that was the place to go—it was as if that was where the store was supposed to be. The light was her sign to do it. The next day, Dee and Rachel called and asked to change to the new unit and were able to do everything very easily. They never had any problems getting the shop up and running.

Gentry Square is said to have been moved into Old Town Spring and once used as a boys' school. There have been numerous sightings of spirits walking around. A little boy hangs out by the light pole, looking for his mother. A female spirit is said to help bring business to shop owners. *Author's collection.*

As she started going into the shop every day, Dee came into contact with a female spirit. She described it as being around thirty-five years old. I've always seen her as a woman dressed in white with her hair up in a bun, as may have been done in the period when Old Town Spring was booming. She was wearing a period dress. She always felt calm and peaceful whenever she felt this female spirit's presence there. There were certain things the spirit liked. Whenever Dee had colorful flowers in the shop, people would comment. People would even comment when the flowers weren't there.

Dee would go into the shop to spiritually cleanse the store and get ready for the day. She would joke around and ask the lady spirit to help her out and go out and bring those people who need my help. Rachel would laugh and say, "Do you really think she is going to bring them in?" People started telling Dee that they would be in Wunsche eating and would follow a trail of pennies to the store. They would tell Dee that they needed to come that way and then would see the sign; they didn't know why, but they had to go into the store. Many times, these new clients were struggling and just needed positive energy, or they had a gift. Dee believed this was a helpful spirit for her shop looking out for her.

Three years later, Dee and Rachel opened a second shop in historic Lewisburg, Pennsylvania. A gifted woman came in one day for a reading, and they became friends. The new friend told Dee, "'I've got to tell you something. There is a woman that surrounds you all the time.' She described her exactly the way I see her. Then she told me that she wants you to know that she's with you and she's around you. The day before I got this call we had just moved into the new location in Old Town Spring and I was feeling bad and even perhaps guilty that I was leaving my helpful ghost behind that I had become accustomed to having around."

This call made Dee feel much better. The next day, the friend called again and told her, "I had a dream about the lady and she is me in a past life." It made sense for her because, for some reason, many of the people coming into the shop in Old Town Spring would talk about being from Lewisburg or having some connection to the town of Lewisburg in Pennsylvania.

After Dee and Rachel moved into the new building, they were waiting for one of the utilities to be turned on one day. They were in the middle of construction, and it was hot in the building. Dee decided to go visit the Spring Historical Museum across the street and walk around in some cool air. She found the photograph of the woman who had been following her around.

Another thing happened while Dee was in her store. One day, her niece was visiting her from Toronto. She also has spiritual gifts, including being a sensitive and medium. They were sitting on the porch when her niece started staring at a spot in the courtyard, Dee she asked, "What are you looking at?" She told her, "I'm looking at that little boy. He is lost and he is looking for his momma." She said, "He is about ten years old and he is standing by that light pole in between Ellen's and the main building right over there. He lost his mom and he is waiting for his mom to come back. He hangs around over there because not too far from there he lost her, and I don't think he's gone."

ELLEN'S CAFÉ

307 Gentry Street
Spring, TX 77373

According to the Harris County Appraisal District, a portion of this building was constructed in 1937; the other part was added in 1997. It has a total of 3,073 square feet of space. As seen from the front, it looks like a cute little cottage. Inside, one can see how far back it actually goes.

Matthew and Jessica Dollinger Lynn are the current owners and have been in the building since May 2015. They are both chefs and met in culinary school. They serve homemade breakfast, lunch and dinner with a variety of sandwiches, soups, quiches, salads and gourmet Akaushi beef hamburgers. They also have homemade ice cream, desserts and fudge. They upload images every day of their menu offerings on Facebook.

Jessica told me that she has been seeing things out of the corner of her left eye in the downstairs area. She will be working and see someone or something move in her peripheral vision. She turns, thinking it's a customer that she may need to help, but nobody is there. It can be startling to see nothing there when you know for a fact you saw something. She believes the ghost is a man named Henry, a former railroad worker.

> *It is an actual figure. Sometimes, things will relocate themselves. At times, I know that something is put in a spot, but when I look again it's no longer there.*

Ellen's Café is located at 307 Gentry Street. The spirit of a man named Henry is said to live in the space. Sometimes employees get him a cup of coffee and leave a note for him to read so that he will be at peace and let them work. *Author's collection.*

Lauren Matney told me about her experiences working at Ellen's Café:

> *I park in the back of my building and one day I was walking to work. I walk down the side of the building where the two buildings meet. I saw a dark, shadowy person. It looked like a real person walking down the stairs at the same pace that I was walking right alongside the building. It looked like a man, and I looked over and he disappeared. I looked to say like "Good morning," but they disappeared and I knew for sure that they were there but then all of a sudden, they were not there. I got really creeped out, so I ran into work.*

I have heard stories from a multitude of people who tell me that they see someone walking, but that the person then disappears. It seems to happen frequently around this area of town. Jessica told me:

> *In the kitchen, I was alone getting some soups together and I felt something reach and grab right here underneath my knee. I turned to look, and there was nobody there. It wasn't like a hard, aggressive squeeze. It was just like*

a normal squeeze. It was really weird! The blood felt like it rushed out of my face, and I ran out of the kitchen. There are two other ladies who work here, Taylor and Blanca, and they also have stories from the years they have worked here. One day they were in the soup area where I was, and they saw the table move, which looked like the table literally jumped. For a while, we had these letters that would spell "E A T." They would light up, and they had a cord connected. We cut the cord because the batteries died, and we just wanted to arrange them somewhere else. When we would come in for work, we would notice the letters would be rearranged to "T E A," and the letters were by where we serve tea.

Jessica told me that the letters have now been attached to the wall. It was too weird finding the letters always rearranged.

As you walk in now they are attached to the wall right there. If they changed now it would be really something. It was about a solid two-week period of time they moved before we put them on the wall. It was almost daily and our little metal teapots would fall off the shelf in the kitchen. His name is Henry and he is a figure. I see what looks like a solid figure. Pat

Interior of Ellen's Café, where a man plays with letters, rearranging them from "EAT" to "TEA." He used to love coffee, but now it's all about the tea. He is said to sometimes knock the little metal teapots off the shelf in the kitchen. *Author's collection.*

> *from Celtic Odyssey came in one day and tapped into the energy here and gave him a name, it was Henry, and she gave us his background. She said "for some reason he likes coffee." So, for a while then we were setting out a cup of coffee and leaving a note for him, because for a while he was just being a little too active. We would be like "we are trying to get something done around here Henry here's a cup of coffee is this going to make you happy" for a while and then he switched to liking tea.*

I asked Lauren if she was ever scared to be in the building. She pointed to the parlor as the front room that has glass separating it from the rest of the restaurant, where the ice cream and fudge are sold. She said, "Sometimes, when I'm alone in the parlor and its quiet. I feel weird sometimes."

While interviewing members of the staff at Ellen's, I was running an audio recorder to make it easier for me to remember all the stories that they told me. After going home and replaying the interview, I found an intelligent electronic voice phenomenon (EVP) of a spirit saying "Yea" in response to a story I was telling someone. I also heard what sounds like chickens in the background, a cat, a moan, singing and a scream.

SCHOOLHOUSE

219 Gentry Street
Spring, TX 77373

One of the rumors about this building, erected in 1950 and comprising 5,026 square feet, is that it had been an old army barracks before it came to Old Town Spring. The owner of the Dugout in Doering Court, Sharon Richardson, told me that she taught school for many years in the Aldine School District in this very building. She taught science, math, health and physical education for the sixth, seventh and eighth grades. Sharon told me that after she left teaching and started building her business in Old Town Spring, the schoolhouse building that she used to work in was moved next to her property. She laughed when she told me she thought the building may be following her.

It was moved to Old Town Spring in the early 1980s, perhaps 1983 or '84. Sharon told me she was standing in her front yard watching when the building came rolling down the street. I am sure that was quite a sight.

When the schoolhouse was in its glory days, it was located in the Aldine district, behind the original administration building on Aldine Westfield Road. Sometime around 1973, the Aldine School District added the chiller and cooling tower to cool the buildings. Just imagine what it was like with no air-conditioning. Calgofo said:

I can tell you what it was like. It was hotter than hell. You sweated all day and your hands and forearms stuck to any paper you were writing on. Sweat would drip off your face and cause spots on your paper. The smell was a combination of perspiration and old chalk dust. It was miserable but, in my case, it wasn't much better at home. We had a window unit but were too poor to run it that often. When the temperature would get up into the mid-nineties, my mother would wait 'til I got home, which was usually about three or so. She would close off the living room, which is where our unit was, and would turn it on and by six, it was off. Man, do I remember how wonderful that felt. I lived for those couple of hours. After six, we just used fans 'til the next day. Even to this day I can't sleep without the noise of a fan. I swore then and there I would make something of myself so I could afford A/C at least.

Since the building has been in Old Town Spring, interesting photos have been taken around it over the years. Someone took a photograph of what appears to be a female standing on the porch at night. One night, a paranormal team was investigating in Old Town Spring. They were

The Schoolhouse, located at 219 Gentry Street, was moved to town in the early 1980s from Aldine Independent School District. A woman is sometimes seen and photographed on the front porch of the school. Nobody knows who she is, but one minute she is there, and the next she is gone. *Author's collection.*

randomly taking photographs and running other equipment. When they got back home and started reviewing their collected data, they discovered a woman in one of the photographs. There was nobody on the porch at that time or anywhere around them while they were investigating. The photo was so clear in its depiction of a real person.

Over the years, there have been many captures of spirits in photos. One of the most famous of these is that of the Tulip Staircase Ghost. On Sunday, June 19, 1966, a retired reverend named Ralph Hardy took an interesting photograph while on vacation. He was at the National Maritime Museum in Greenwich, England. The photograph shows the tulip staircase, the first of its kind in Britain. Work started on the house where the staircase is located in 1616 then stopped for a time and was completed in 1636. The home is located in the Queen's House section of the Upon development. After returning home, Hardy developed the film and was shocked to see what appeared to be a hooded figure climbing the stairs while holding on to the railing with both hands. No one was present when he took the photograph. The stairs were even blocked with a chain across it and a sign that read "No admittance."

It is said that if you look closely, you can see what may be two spirits in the photo. Both of the hands seem to be left hands, and there are what look like wedding rings. The negatives were given to experts at Kodak to examine. No evidence was found of tampering or manipulation. In 1967, Reverend Hardy tried to re-create the photograph in the same location with the assistance of the museum photographer. This attempt was not successful.

I have heard stories about other anomalies being caught on film around the schoolhouse. Rowan Dark from After Dark Tours told me a story about a couple of girls who were taking selfies on the side of the schoolhouse. In the images, it appears that only part of them are exposed. In other words, it looked as if they were disappearing.

If you look across the street, you will see the Little Dutch Girl shop. There are stories of the chairs outside moving around. The thought is that one of the town's spirits didn't like the way the shop workers arranged them, so they arranged the chairs in a way they wanted. There is a story of the owner saying the chairs have even been found on top of the building when employees come to open the shop in the morning.

The Dugout

211-S Midway Street
Spring, TX 77373

The Dugout has anything that you can put a logo on, including all kinds of memorabilia and autographed items. It sells freezer mugs, coffee mugs, monster mugs, thermal mugs, blankets, backpacks, wastebaskets, ice buckets, lamps, clocks, car mats, steering wheel covers and headrest covers. This old barn was part of the childhood homestead of Judge Henry Doering and was built by his father, Henry C. Doering, and his mother, Ella Klein, in the early 1900s. At the time of this writing, Doering Court is where you can find the Shabby Rose, Connie's Bath Shack, Susie's and the Dugout. Doering Court is close to the old red schoolhouse on Gentry Street.

There is said to be a spirit named Sarah who haunts this part of town. People report hearing laughing, noises on the roof, voices and the sounds of children playing. They also describe the feeling of being scratched, feeling a rush of cold air or cold spots, experiencing the feeling of being watched and seeing strange lights in the loft and objects moving. Photos taken in the area sometimes contain anomalies that cannot be explained.

Randy Woods, a former assistant press secretary to President Gerald Ford, started the first ghost tour in Old Town Spring, in 1999. He called it the Walking Ghost and History Tour of Old Town Spring and started it in what he called the former barn. He said he had never thought about ghosts until he moved into the shop that has since been taken over by the Dugout. After

The Dugout in Doering Court, located at 211 Midway, is part of the Doering homestead. This is the barn that Sara fell from, injuring her leg. This led to her death sometime later. She is said to haunt the location with some of her other friends. *Author's collection.*

moving into the building, he was working alone late one August night in his office. He heard three claps, felt cold wind and then saw his ficus tree begin to shake. It was hot outside and not windy, so these were strange experiences. In a short period of time, he reported hearing playful sounds and sharp noises on the roof. The noises sounded more like running children than scampering squirrels. In an interview with the *Houston Chronicle*, he said, "I'm a newspaper guy. I'm accustomed to dealing with facts. You've got to experience something like this before you finally say to yourself something unusual is occurring that can't be explained. I was a skeptic, if anything. Like most people, I heard some stories and listened to them pleasantly, then went on about my business. You've got to be around it. Then you start to ask yourself questions."

He started researching what was happening, learning about the area and talking to other business owners. This led him to start the haunted walking tour. Research about the building his business was in indicated that it was the original barn, now known as the Dugout, in the back corner of the courtyard, still on the property. In the 1930s, Henry Doering's youngest daughter, Marilyn, and her twelve-year-old friend Sarah used to play in and around the barn. One day while playing hide-and-seek in the barn, Sarah fell from the loft, breaking her leg. An infection set in, poisoning her blood and eventually causing her death following a few months of suffering. It is said that she still plays in the barn with other young spirits.

Randy Woods believed that young Sarah's spirit returned here because she had spent so many days having fun and playing. She was waiting for her playmates to join her, and it seems that perhaps some have. Several tenants of the building have reported hearing noises of children's laughter and even of hearing the name "Sarah" being called out. Randy said that he believed Sarah and her friends would watch him work late at night. He would come to work in the morning and find things on his desk moved, and he always felt cold spots. "It's an eerie feeling. Sometimes, I feel a rush of cold air around me for no apparent reason. Sometimes when I open the office in the morning. I know that things on my desk have been rearranged, and I have this sensation that the spirit, or whatever it might be, is friendly and means no harm."

Spirit Realm Researchers, led by Linda Houle, spent a night in the building to investigate when it housed the newspaper office. She wrote an

This photograph is looking at the Dugout from the parking lot. It is said that not far from this location was a Ferris wheel, from which a little boy is rumored to have fallen to his death. His spirit is seen at times looking for his mother while the spirit of a man looks for the boy. *Author's collection.*

article about their experiences and even videotaped their stay. Randy used to show some of this video footage during his tours. The video shows what the team thought was the presence of some form of energy and what sounds like children bouncing a ball on the tape. They believed it to be Sarah. Among the things that happened during the investigation were a door closing by itself, the sounds of giggling, the presence of cold spots and a sense of pressure in the air. The team set toys in the loft, hoping to catch them being played with. During most of the night, Linda felt waves of cold air going by her where she was seated. She felt that Sarah may have been hanging around her instead of playing with the toys.

Walking around to the other side of the barn, one stands in the parking lot of Preservation Park, where fairs are set up. Once many years ago, a child passed away here after falling out of a Ferris wheel. You are not too far from the back of the Cake Faery. As you stand here, does the energy feel different to you than it does by the Cake Faery?

Shabby Rose

211 Midway Street
Spring, TX 77373

Today, this shop offers cottage- and flea market–style decor, furniture and accessories, as well as French and European linens and furnishings. This lovely white house is the home of Doering Court and was the childhood home of Judge Doering. The property was originally owned by Charles Wunsche, who sold it to M.E. Hamilton. The next owners were Henry C. Doering and his wife, Ella Klein. One record shows that the home was built in 1911. The property was named Doering Court.

Henry Doering passed away from pneumonia in 1940, leaving behind his wife and four children, one of whom would grow up to become Judge Vernon Doering in Old Town Spring. To take care of her family, Ella started renting the upstairs part of home to railroad workers. She raised her children and lived in this home until her death thirty-three years later. Ella's son Vernon was the last justice of the peace in Spring. In the 1960s and '70s, he worked out of the new courtroom in what is now the Spring Historical Museum.

Local rumors make it seem as though the people who lived here were mean-spirited; that just isn't so. It is said that the tree behind the house, close to the barn, was used to hang people. Judge Doering would sentence someone to hang, oversee the execution on that tree and then go inside to eat dinner while watching the condemned hang there. One story claimed

The Shabby Rose in Doering Court is located at 211 Midway. It is the former childhood home of Judge Vernon Doering. After Judge Doering's father passed away, his mother, Ella, rented out the upstairs to railroad workers. Today, a man is seen moving around upstairs through the windows at certain times. Is he a former railroad worker? *Author's collection.*

that this infamous judge was known worldwide for more than one hundred hangings from the tree in his backyard and that he would leave the body of an executed prisoner in the tree for days to send a signal to others to obey the law in Spring. According to every local historian whom I have spoken with, including the owner of the property, Sharon Richardson, this simply is not true.

Judge Vernon Doering oversaw the court in the 1960s and '70s. There are no historical documents indicating that he brought people to his mother's house to be hanged or even that he sentenced anyone to die. Hangings did not happen in Spring and certainly did not happen outside of someone's home. The tree located on the back of the lot hasn't been on the property for very long. Several historians have told me that there was never a hanging tree in the town. Criminals were sent by train to Houston for trial, and sentences were carried out there.

There were said to be two legal hangings in Houston as soon as the first city court was convened. The men were promptly hanged outside the court. The first documented legal hanging in Houston was of a man named Hyde in 1853 in a place known as Hangman's Grove on the southeast corner of a cemetery on San Felipe Road. Today, the location is in Founder's Cemetery on West Dallas Street. There is a tree, known as the Old Hanging Tree, located on Bagby Street by Buffalo Bayou with a plaque that reads:

> *Many stories attached to the 400-year-old history of this live oak. Some say that, during the days of the Republic of Texas (1836–1845), at least eleven criminals were hanged from its graceful boughs. Although others dispute the tales, the legend survives.*
>
> *In 1896 a courthouse with jail was built nearby. Inside, criminals were hanged from scaffolds. Outside, beneath this tree, relatives, mourners, and onlookers gathered and waited.*
>
> *A second courthouse building later occupied the site. When it was demolished in the 1960's to make room for the Albert Thomas Convention Center, a basement wall was left intact to protect the tree's root system.*
>
> *The Old Hanging Tree is thought by some to be the oldest tree in Harris County.*
>
> *Today the Old Hanging Tree is maintained and preserved by the City of Houston Civic Center Department.*

The first recorded legal execution in the entire state of Texas occurred in 1819, when George Brown was put to death for piracy. Prior to Texas statehood in 1846, there were eight legal executions by hanging. After statehood, hanging would be the method used for almost all Texas executions until 1924. The last hanging in the state was that of Nathan Lee, who was convicted of murder and executed on August 31, 1923. A total of 390 legal hangings were conducted in the state. Lynching, on the other hand, claimed 468 victims in Texas between 1885 and 1942.

Perhaps the many psychic impressions of hangings on this property date back to a time before the area was even known as Camp Spring and before a judge had lived here for part of his life. Stories over time can twist and be amended, as everyone knows. And some things are completely made up. Perhaps a lynching did take place somewhere in Old Town Spring.

At the Shabby Rose, there have been reports of a shadowy figure looking out from the upstairs windows when nobody is in the house. In addition, some photographs show someone looking out from one of the windows. Could this be one of the railroad workers who lived upstairs? Some photographs taken of the tree show anomalies. Are the spirits in the area hanging out in this tree so they can be seen on photos? Maybe these anomalies are related to Sarah and the kids who are said to play in this area.

Indigo Hair Studio

26303 Preston Avenue
Spring, TX 77373

Today, the Indigo Hair Studio offers highly trained professional hair services, including cuts, styling, coloring and aromatherapy treatments. It is also a Brazilian blowout certified salon. Property records indicate that this building was constructed in 1930. The owner of Indigo Hair Studio, Jenny Burroughs Wright, told me, "At the salon, we've had multiple items fly off shelves. Once a couple of years ago, I saw a ten-pound object levitate in midair and then fall. No actual spirit or apparition has ever been seen, but there is definitely the feeling. It mostly seems to happen in one room in the salon. I have spoken to previous owners, and they seemed to have a lot more issues than we have had in the last three years."

Jenny told me that since the building has become home to Indigo, clients have said that they haven't seen anything strange. It would certainly be neat to both get your hair done and see something unusual, like a ghost. Former owners of the shop have told Jenny stories about their experiences. "When the pet store was here, apparently, the dog cages would be opened every night. The lady that owned the bookstore in here years back said that she would hear a music box playing, loud footsteps and stacks of books would go flying across the room."

Diana Diamond, who owns the building next to Indigo, talks about her husband seeing and talking to the ghost, a little girl named Shelly. They have

At Indigo, a hair salon located at 26303 Preston Street, resides the spirit of a little girl named Shelby. She has been around for years, moving things around and unlocking the cages of animals that once lived in the former pet store. *Author's collection.*

been in this area for many years and know all about the activity that happens here. Sometimes, spirits show themselves at an age when they were happiest in life, but that doesn't mean that they passed away at that age. The little girl who lives here could be an older spirit.

In several of the cases we have worked over the years, activity has been tied to a very small space in a business or home. Workers in one large warehouse noticed things moving around only within ten feet of a desk. The chair would spin, things would fly off the desk and items would be knocked over. We don't have a scientific explanation. We feel that these are pockets of high energy. It could be that the spirit is attached to an object in the center of the activity. In some cases, if you can pinpoint what the object is, you can get rid of the haunting. We have had multiple cases in which activity took place because of changes in the environment. To keep everything calm, the solution is to keep everything the same.

Some of these types of hauntings involve what we label a poltergeist. This German word is translated as "noisy ghost." Different levels of paranormal activity may be associated with a poltergeist. Unusual physical phenomena characterize this type of haunting—doors opening and closing, banging sounds, moving objects, knocking, fires and the appearance of strange pools of water. Most of the cases we have dealt with regarding this type of activity usually involve a young girl of twelve to sixteen years of age. We believe the activity can be a manifestation of psychokinesis. Science has not yet fully understood the mind and what it is capable of. The teenager becomes upset, and somehow, the anger permeates the atmosphere, creating this type of haunting.

Sometimes, noisy ghosts are there just to get attention, to make themselves known or until a solution for their problem is figured out. People have been known to be injured by the activity. In many of these cases, the activity was directed to a person—as if the spirit didn't like that person. Nobody at this location has reported a personal attack, but the activity sounds as if a poltergeist is present.

Crazy Mama's

26303 Preston Street
Spring Texas 77373

Diana Diamond owns Crazy Mama's in what is called the "Courtyard of the Angels" on Preston Street. She recently moved from the pink building and into another one in the same courtyard. Paranormal activity has already started up again. She wanted me to know how active the cottages and courtyard were. People see orbs with their own eyes all the time, and there is a little girl who is very active but has never done anything mean-spirited. Diana said:

> *The most recent thing that happened was about a year ago. Pam, who is a friend of mine, came to the shop to help me do some stuff. She took a picture of the front of the shop and texted it to me to say, "Hey, I'm here waiting." The picture looks like it moved a little bit when she took it. She caught a blue spirit in that picture, and I have it on my phone. It was like a blue ethereal spirit that floated right in front of her in front of the shop. It's the same blue that represents the Archangel Michael. That's who I always call on to fight my battles for me. The spirit that I told you about, her name is Shelly. She is young, I would say probably eight years old, or something like that. She isn't a recent spirit, because she goes back to the Civil War days. I think it's kind of unusual for someone from that day and time to have the name Shelly.*

This a photograph of the Courtyard of the Angels. You can see most of the buildings that have reported activity by a very mischievous little girl. The building on the right side of the walkway was most recently Crazy Mama's. *Author's collection.*

Mark, a friend of Diana's, has had a shop in Old Town Spring in different locations, including in the middle of the back of the courtyard. That site is now a dog grooming establishment. When he worked out of the building, his shop sold clocks and other items. Lots and lots of clocks, according to Diana. Every day, Mark and his employees would come in and make sure that all of the clocks were set and working correctly. The spirit of this little girl, which now lives around here, would come in every night and change the time on every clock. When they came in, all the clocks would be set at 10:10. She seems to be a very mischievous little girl. Mark had another store, next to his clock shop. It is today the Indigo Hair Salon. At this store, Mark sold exotic animals, which were kept in cages. The little girl would open the cages during the night. Diana believes there are still exotic animals running around in the courtyard.

> *When we first moved to Old Town Spring, which was over seven and a half years ago now, the Indigo building was empty. We were storing stuff in there as we painted and got things set up in our building. My husband, who used to be a non-believer of the paranormal, was taking some stuff*

between buildings, between the Indigo and the dog grooming place, and he saw something move. He was taking some stuff to lean against the fence. Something flashed by on the right of him, and when he turned to look, nothing was there. He paid no attention to it, but when he came back, it happened again, and this time, he could tell that it was a little girl. This courtyard is very active.

When Diana first moved to the pink cottage, things would randomly be thrown off the shelves every day. That's when Mark told them about Shelly.

So, I had a come-to-Jesus meeting with her and told her, "Look, we are going to be here for a while, we are going to have a good time, and you're going to love it. We respect you and we just hope that you respect us and you respect that we have a business to run here." We have never had any problems since then. Now that we moved in the new building, that's changed. We had a group of people who were helping us move and set up. One of the pictures, which is a painting of a cat, was just hung on the northwest wall of the perfume salon. We heard a "boom" sound, and the cat picture had come off, like lifted up and off the hook and come down.

I was told that a multitude of the cottages around Old Town Spring had been moved in from the Heights. Diana told me that she believed that whoever used to live in the houses and had passed away somehow has reconnected. Many years ago, there was a woman who walked all over Old Town Spring. She was gifted in a metaphysical sense. She said there was

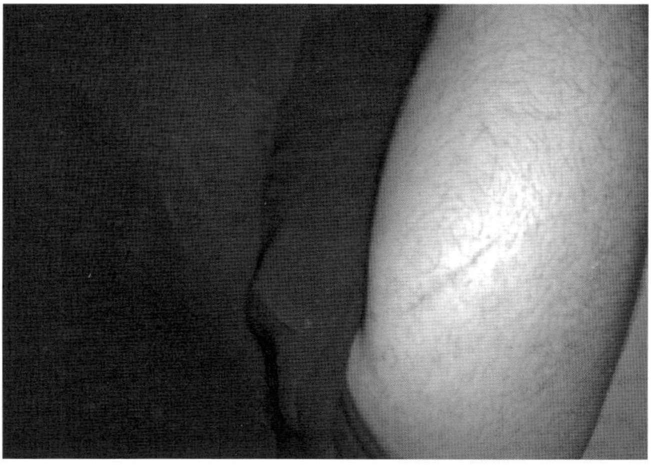

This scratch occurred while Woodlands Paranormal was investigating. Sometimes spirits can scratch to let you know they are there. *Author's collection.*

something like ley lines crossing in the whole area. She said that Old Town Spring was built over a metaphysical grid.

It is interesting to note that there have been multiple buildings brought in from the Heights to Old Town Spring. A millionaire named Oscar Martin Carter, along with other investors, established a company by 1891 that bought 1,756 acres of land. They called it Houston Heights. It was accessible by streetcar for those people who did not want live in the busy city. By the 1970s, the area had fallen into disrepair and had become a low-income suburb of Houston.

A sadistic serial killer named Dean Corll, also known as the "Candy Man," was on the loose in Houston Heights beginning on December 13, 1970. He lured and killed at least twenty-eight children. He befriended two twelve-year-old boys, David Brooks and Elmer Wayne Henley, who helped lure more children to him. All of his known victims were boys between the ages of twelve and twenty. Perhaps the high emotions generated by the horrors of what Corll was doing were imprinted onto the buildings before they were moved. Many places where strong emotions occur are said to be haunted.

CELTIC ODYSSEY

123 Midway Street
Spring, TX 77373

This 1,504-square-foot building, erected in 1914, houses a retail shop. Owners Darkforest Ivy and Robert Griffin Dutkiewicz specialize in Celtic-themed products; Renaissance clothing and accessories; Celtic music; magic supplies; soaps; natural products and candles; antiques and artisan works, such as Celtic art; fairy cages; and homemade wooden items, such as rocking horses, pens and cutting boards. It is said that a ghost occupies the space. A female spirit is believed to be in this location—the energy is very feminine, according to Rowan Dark with After Dark Ghost Tours. This spirit also likes to move things around because nothing is where store employees put it the night before. Rowan said, "When you come into the Celtic Odyssey, we would like you to say 'Hi, Sydney' because she seems to be in a lot better mood when you acknowledge her."

In the same courtyard stand the post office building and a gazebo. It is said that a random green light or orb hangs around in this area. It will sometimes dance around certain people. It has been seen with the naked eye and captured in photographs, as well. Tour guides encourage people to take as many photographs as they can in an attempt to catch the image.

The gazebo in the courtyard also seems to have some type of paranormal activity associated with it. The store employees believe that there is some kind of a portal or gate where the gazebo stands. Some people who walk

The Celtic Odyssey Emporium and Spa is located at 123 Midway. The ghost of a woman named Sydney lives here. She wants you to say, "Hi, Sydney" when you come in the store. *Author's collection.*

through or sit in the space are said to get nauseous; others feel like they are spinning. I sat for a time myself in the gazebo and felt light-headed. I will have to go back there and spend quality time sitting in the gazebo while running equipment to see what is there. The owners of the Celtic Odyssey don't know if this activity is related to the spirt that they are calling Sydney, but they say "it's definitely there according to several psychics."

About five years ago, Rowan was conducting a tour and happened to notice that everyone who walked through the space felt sick. One of them even got smacked in the face by an unseen force, producing a red mark. Someone thought that perhaps a spirit or something similar was trying to keep the visitors from encountering something evil.

Perhaps the energy is what we call a vortex—a concentrated energy center that has the potential to be tapped into. Vortices contain a spiraling type of energy. This could explain the feeling of dizziness some visitors experienced. Sensations people claim to experience at this site include tingling, vibrations and something like pressure across the back and neck. Spirits can be attracted to places like this. It's said that this attraction is like a candle in the darkness to them.

This post office building is known for a green light that likes to hover around certain people. *Author's collection.*

Another theory is that spirits need energy to manifest things into happening. People can be attracted to these energy centers and may use them for healing or prayer. Sedona, Arizona, is an example. It has been called a spiritual Disneyland. It hosts several of the many known vortices around the world. When you are in Old Town Spring, come sit in the gazebo and see for yourself if you are able to feel the energy.

Masterpiece Handcrafted Furniture

119 Midway Street
Spring, TX 77373

While on a ghost tour, I was told that this place was always called the "cat house" and that the front porch is said to have a ghost dog. The rocking horse that used to sit on the porch would sometimes rock by itself before it was removed. People would report seeing it rock at different times of the day and night. I was told that this is one of the oldest buildings in Old Town Spring. Around the corner, in the courtyard next door to the Celtic Odyssey, you will find the main location of Masterpiece Handcrafted Furniture. You can see its handcrafted custom tables, hutches, buffets and chairs, but its building on Midway Street is empty.

The property was purchased by the parents of Jenny Burroughs Wright, who owns the Indigo Hair Studio. After purchasing the Midway location, they began to renovate the old building, which was in need of extensive repair. Apparently, whatever was in the building did not like the changes being made, so the worker they hired got a taste of the paranormal. Many times, people don't believe in the paranormal until something unexplained happens to them, in which case they know they had a personal experience. I wonder what the worker thought. Jenny told me, "Once sometime last year, there was a man underneath, trying to level the building, and some kind of force picked up his legs and moved him. That sounded a little sinister, but nothing like we have ever experienced at the salon."

An old house that is located at 119 Midway. I was told it was one of the oldest original houses in Spring. It is owned by Masterpiece Handcrafted Furniture. There was a man who was yanked by an unseen force under the building while he was working here. There is also the spirit of a dog that is sometimes seen on the porch. *Author's collection.*

Midway Street looking east at the depot before it was destroyed. On the right of the photo are Wunsche Brothers and Townsend Mercantile, owned by Alec Klein, who sold coffins in the corner of his store. On the right is the spot where the Spotted Pony would eventually be moved to. Photograph taken in the early 1900s. *Courtesy Spring Historical Museum.*

A good example of an intelligent haunting in which things are thrown around by a "ghost" is the Bell Witch case in Adams, Tennessee. The haunting activity occurred from 1817 to 1821. The haunting began when John Bell had an encounter with a strange animal in a cornfield. The animal, resembling a dog and a rabbit, disappeared when he shot at it. The activity then started in earnest and included knocking, rapping noises, scratching sounds, blankets pulled from beds and people being scratched and their hair pulled. John's daughter Elizabeth got the brunt of much of the activity—she was slapped, pinched, bruised and stuck with pins. Many people witnessed the activity; some of them would come and camp out on the property. The Bell Witch was so well known that General Andrew Jackson, who later became president, came for a visit and had his own personal experiences.

Spring State Bank

115 Midway
Spring, TX 77373

On May 19, 1910, Spring, Texas, with a population of approximately twelve hundred people, saw the Spring State Bank established with approximately $10,000 and one hundred shares of stock. The bank was in a wooden structure on Main Street, the current location of Puffabelly's. It burned down on December 6, 1917. The fire started in a barn and destroyed the bank, a residence and a rental house owned by Mr. Brady. The vault and its contents were saved intact from the old building, and the bank was rebuilt in its current location. Brick was used for the reconstruction, but it wasn't enough to keep out the robbers. The bank operated at its current location until 1935, when it consolidated with Guarrenty Bond State Bank in Tomball. I talked to owner David Mallott, who told me:

> *It was a doctor's office at one time and at least two babies were born in here. It was also a barbershop at one time, and I got my first big boy haircut right over here. It had a low ceiling I could reach up and touch then. About 1975, I came home from something and my dad said, "There is an electrical problem. Get up there and see what you can find." I had a flashlight and said, "Dad, you need to take down this drop ceiling, because there is a beadboard ceiling up there." So, we took it out and opened it up.*

There were several robberies in the history of the town, including one on May 24, 1932, and another on January 6, 1933. There were six shots fired inside the bank and six shots fired outside during one of the robberies. Another one of the robberies was said to have been committed by a couple of men, with Clyde Barrow being positively identified by several people. After they fled, the robbers met up with a few women, one of whom resembled Bonnie Parker. Whoever it was, they got away with $7,380. It was never confirmed that they were in fact the famous Bonnie and Clyde; many doubt the rumors that it was really them. There are many tales throughout Texas of the famed duo robbing a place or sleeping somewhere.

Barrow had been tied to the Houston area, which could include Old Town Spring. An article in the old *Houston Post* reported that Barrow joined the Root Square Gang in Houston's Fifth Ward, where he started a life of crime—at the time, merely a series of petty thefts. Eventually, his criminal activity escalated to robbing grocery stores and gas stations before he met Parker in January 1930 and fell in love. On April 21, 1930, he became prisoner #63527 in Eastham Prison Farm at 2665 Prison Road #1, thirteen miles east of Trinity. He was given a fourteen-year sentence.

The Old Bank, located at 115 Midway, is called Mallott's today. It is the site of one of the supposed Bonnie and Clyde robberies. The spirit of a man haunts this place; some say he is looking for his money. You can still see numerous places in the façade where bullets ricocheted from past robberies. *Author's collection.*

This was a brutal place for anyone. The inmates did hard labor, and the guards were merciless. It was here that Barrow added murder to his list of crimes. Ed Crowder, also known as "Big Ed," was six feet tall and weighed two hundred pounds. The story is that he had repeatedly taken advantage of Barrow, so Barrow stabbed him fifteen times. Barrow had a fellow convict chop off two of his toes with an axe—part of his plan to escape. He was then moved to the prison in Huntsville and was granted an early parole. When Barrow got out of prison in February 1932, he hooked up again with Bonnie, and the famous duo got back into their life of crime, along with the other Barrow Gang members, Marvin and Blanche Barrow, Raymond Hamilton, Ralph Fultz, William D. Jones, Joe Palmer and Henry Methvin. On their notorious crime spree, they robbed grocery stores, filling stations and small banks. They killed at least nine police officers and at least four civilians before being ambushed and killed by law officers on a rural road in Bienville Parish, Louisiana. The parish coroner, Dr. J.L. Wade, gave a detailed autopsy report in 1934. It showed that Clyde Barrow had seventeen separate entrance wounds; Bonnie Parker had twenty-six entrance wounds. At the Texas Prison Museum in Huntsville is a nickel-plated Colt .45 that was on Parker's lap at the time the duo was ambushed.

When you walk up to the old bank building today, you can see where bullets ricocheted or left holes in the façade during one of the attempted robberies. The holes were made by a trio of felons who were unsuccessful in getting any money from the bank. I was told by the owner of the property that the largest hole, which actually looks like a hole as opposed to a ricochet on the building, was drilled by his dad when he was trying to install an awning. He was standing there helping his dad and watching him drill it. I have heard that attempts have been made to patch the holes, but the patches won't stay in place and fall out.

> *My mom bought it because my dad's store was next door and she wanted her own little thing. She was a florist and had a bunch of stuff and she said she wanted her own shop. She bought this building in 1963 for $2,500. She is eighty-five years old today. I asked her, "Momma, why did you buy this building?" She told me it was because she didn't want anybody else to have it. The hardware store was next door and she wanted it to be kind of tied together.*

Owner David Mallott showed me an old flyer from Mallott's store that was found by a friend of his in a barn that they were tearing down off Riley

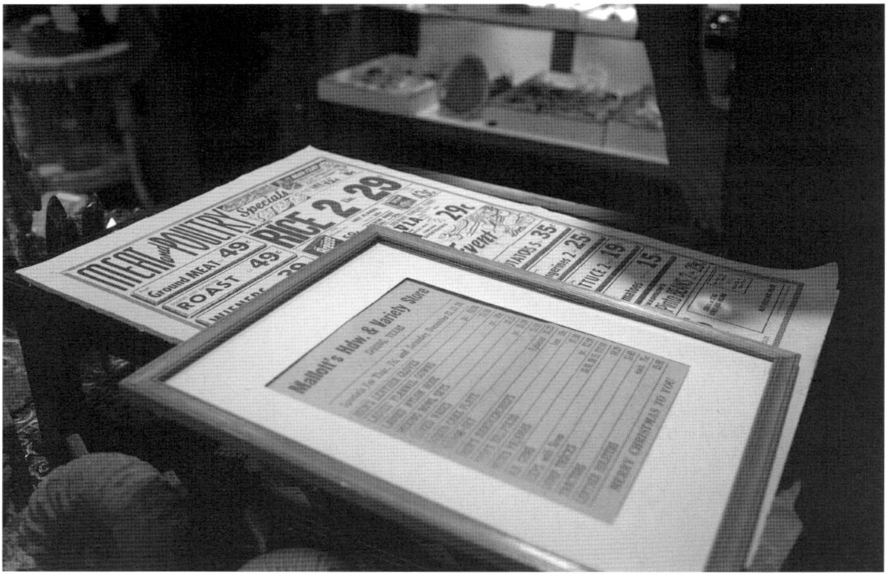

Mallott's Hardware posters, found in an old barn off Riley Ruzzel Road. *Author's collection.*

Fuzzel Road. The friend brought it over to give it to David and told him that he thought that he would like to have this. It was the grocery store flyer, and it had been all bent. David told me, "Grandma used to run off a smaller version of this in the kitchen on a mimeograph machine."

There is an opening in the bank where you walk into another room. This area used to be the alleyway between the hardware store and the bank. In 1973, David's dad enclosed the area because he wanted to have more retail space. It was a kite shop at one time. He told me that he remembers as a kid his dad using the alley to store Christmas trees because it was cool and dark. It always smelled like Christmas trees in here in December.

The owner himself has had some odd things happen in the store. There have been noises upstairs, but no one knows what it is. He had a box of pushpins and lost the last one when it fell out of the case onto the carpet. He crawled around trying to find it so it wouldn't hurt a customer. He moved the rug and furniture and finally gave up looking for it and put everything back. When he came back in the morning, the pushpin was sitting smack dab in the middle of the chair. He though the ghost might have been protecting him.

Photos taken in the old bank sometimes have strange anomalies, some of which look like apparitions. You can even stand across the street and

Left: The bank vault. *Author's collection.*

Below: Side of the bank. *Author's collection.*

get interesting photos of the building. The original vault is still inside the building today. It has a crawlspace over the top of it with four feet of sand. The owner thinks there must be over three thousand pounds of sand up there. You can take a look at it during business hours, depending on who is leasing the building. At this time, the owner of the building is also operating the shop. The store has at times allowed people to walk into the vault. Today, there is a rope blocking the area in order to protect the space, but you can still see the vault.

Psychics who have gone into the vault feel the energy of a man. They say that the energy is awesome in there. They believe this man, who is seen with a big nose, tried to stop the robberies. For whatever reason, over the years, it has been noted that whoever leases the bank doesn't stay for long. Perhaps they have been scared away by something unseen. Some believe that the man who is said to haunt the location is looking for his money and bothers the storekeepers. Maybe the man is being protective of the place. Anomalous photos have been taken. They show what appears to be a man with a big nose.

In November 2005, one team caught a mist while it was forming during an investigation. On another investigation, they captured what they think is an apparition of a man wearing a 1930s hat. You can see an outline of shoulders and what looks like a tall collar and a suit jacket. In October 2013 and again in 2015, Haunted Houston Tours uploaded several videos online with audible voices captured during ghost box sessions outside the building.

The bank building is today named Mallott's Hardware and Variety Store. It offers an ever-changing blend of home decor, art, furniture, rocks, crystals and mineral specimens. You can also buy sage and sweetgrass to cleanse your home. These plants have been long revered for their use in ceremonial purifying, cleansing and warding off evil spirits.

THE SPOTTED PONY

102 Midway Street
Spring, TX 77373

This is one of developer R.I. Robinson's original houses and the first house with indoor plumbing in Old Town Spring. The house was originally located on Main Street and was moved to its current location. In October 2000, the paranormal team Ghost Hunters of Southeast Texas (GHOST) investigated the Spotted Pony after hearing claims from the owner, Shirley Clayton. That night, they captured a few anomalies, including a shadow person. Shirley likes to talk about the ghosts of her shop as if they are family members. She has had several shops in Old Town Spring, and she believed that one followed her from one place to another. She was interviewed by the *Houston Chronicle*: "I definitely believe there's a ghost in this store. We call him John. He hides my keys sometimes. Sometimes, when I get really frustrated and can't find them, I have to stop and talk to the ghost and he'll ring a bell, or something will happen that will draw me to where my keys are hid."

When Shirley was originally in the building, her office was located in a different place than it is now. She would stay there, working late at night. She would clean up her desk; it would be nice, neat and organized. She then would leave to do something in the store. When she walked back into the room, there would be a paperclip in the middle of her desk. She would pick up the paperclip and put it away, then leave again to do something. When she walked back in, another paperclip was on her desk. It was as if they were

The Crawfish Festival draws an estimated fifty thousand annual visitors to Old Town Spring for the food and music. *Author's collection.*

multiplying. She called this the "paperclip game." Shirley was convinced that Charlie had moved with her to the new store location and that, after some time, he left because they burned sage and sweetgrass all the time. She has no idea where he went; perhaps he's back in that store again. Shirley told me:

> *I'm convinced that Charlie moved with me over there, and what would happen is that I would lose my keys. We were a Western store, and I had two mannequins in that store that were Indians. Lots of times, I couldn't find my keys, and I would say, "Charlie, it's 1:00 a.m., and you better find my keys." There would be a noise, and I would hear it and find my keys there. I would go over, and the keys would usually be in one of the Indians' lap. There was a whiskey table with a board set up with checkers, like the Indians were playing them, and I said, "If the keys are in there, you are real." I found the keys in there right after that.*

Shirley had a random experience on another day—she's not sure if it was a spirit or not. She had a bunch of errands to run. While she was out, she kept being pushed in her mind to go back to the shop. She decided to go back and eat in front of the building, but she felt pulled to stop and go into the shed. Following her gut instinct, she went into the shed and found an employee backpack that had all the money in credit card receipts that had been stolen from when Shirley and her employees were at the Houston Livestock Show and Rodeo. The cash was gone but not, thank goodness, the receipts. She walked to her car with the backpack when the employee pulled up who had helped her load everything at the rodeo. If it would have been two minutes earlier, she would have never known about the backpack. Was this a spirit guide, or Charlie helping her find the lost money? He had been helping her find her keys, so it's possible he was involved.

In 1990, there was a one-hundred-year-old antique oak organ from a church in Ireland that Shirley wanted to get, but she happened to be on vacation in New Orleans and had no way to get it. So her parents went to the auction and picked it up for her. They also brought home a framed photo of the little girl that is now hanging in her shop. Her parents told her that the little girl was cute, so they decided to get it for her. The subject of the picture is a young girl. It is hung on the wall at an angle (in a diamond shape) instead of being hung square. On the back, it is dated December 25, 1948. The strange thing was that there was no bid number for the person who had offered the picture of the little girl up for auction and nobody claimed the picture, so Shirley's parents did. This picture had caused Shirley's colleagues to become so uneasy that they said they would not return. Shirley told me, "She came home with me and she was upstairs in our house. I was teaching school at the time in New Caney, sixth-grade English. So she's upstairs and you know she watches you, and I was having a Christmas party. Some of the teachers went upstairs to use the restroom and then they came down and were all upset because of her."

Shirley moved to Tomball by herself, smudged her house with sage and sweetgrass and decided to put the picture up in a closet facing the wall. She didn't want to deal with the little girl alone at the time. She stored the picture until she decided to bring it out and hang it in her store in Old Town Spring. She had moved her shop to 202 Main Street. Randy Woods came in talking about the ghosts of Old Town Spring, and she thought, "You really need to see my little girl one day." She brought the picture to the store and had an employee—later a Houston police department officer—hang it on the wall. The employee took the picture out, and when the employee went to hang it, the girl looked through both Shirley and her

The Loose Caboose is located at 26403 Preston Street. It is a favorite place to grab a bite to eat while shopping. *Author's collection.*

and then smiled. They both looked at each other to make sure they weren't going crazy. Then they realized they really had just both seen her smile. They all believed she was happy to finally be out of storage.

While I was talking with Shirley, she had me walk from one side of the room to the other. It does look like the little girl's eyes moved, like they were following me, and her expression changed. It was slight, but it was enough to know that it did appear to change. Shirley has believed her name to be Sara, but she doesn't know why.

> *One time, we tried having a séance to contact the girl in the photograph; her expression changed then. She was gloomy and very unhappy. I didn't pay much attention to what was said by them. I took it with a grain of salt, because they could have been making things up. She stays with me and seems to be happy here at the shop. People have come in and cried especially at little things with the little girl. People see her expression change and her eyes follow them.*

She is still hanging on the wall and would love for you to visit her. While you are here, the shop offers ladies' fashions, collectibles, jewelry, Renaissance clothing for men and women (including doublets, vests, belts, pirate coats, cloaks, capes, hats and dresses), belly dancer costumes and fairy outfits.

WUNSCHE BROTHERS

103 Midway Street
Spring, TX 77373

The oldest standing commercial structure in Old Town Spring is Wunsche Brothers. Many barroom brawls took place here; beer was sold on tap for five cents a glass. Some stories claim that the structure was built in 1902 by Dell and Willie Wunsche. They are said to haunt the barn. This historic seven-thousand-square-foot building was damaged when a fire started in the bar area on March 29, 2015. At this time, part of the building needs to be rebuilt, and repairs are needed to remedy the smoke damage. It currently has a fence around it to protect it from further damage and to protect the public. It was listed for sale for $450,000 soon after the fire and has recently been sold. The historical marker is still in place and reads: "The Wunsches, one of Spring's earliest families who immigrated from Germany in 1846, constructed this building in 1902. The Wunsche Bros. Saloon and Hotel, later known as the Spring Cafe, was built to accommodate railroad workers and has served as a community gathering place throughout the town's history. The structure, which exhibits typical turn-of-the-century commercial detailing, is Spring's oldest existing commercial building on its original site. (Recorded as a Texas Historic Landmark in 1984.)"

Carl Wunsche Sr. purchased the property that the Wunsche Brothers Restaurant sits on in 1862 from Wiley Smith for a sum of eighty dollars.

Old Wunsche Brothers Saloon, 1902. Irvin T. Wunsche is on the right; second from right is William Wunsche. *Courtesy Spring Historical Museum.*

An existing structure had operated as a café, run by Widow Betty, but it was knocked down by a tornado. The property legally changed hands multiple times within the family before Wunche Brothers was built. E.N. Wunsche was the owner in 1902 when the building was constructed.

In an interview, William "Willie" Wunsche said that the building was actually constructed in the summer of 1902 by William Wunsche Sr., Ralph Hanks, Voress Bonin and Jim Burris. The materials included salvaged wood from the former café as well as unused lumber that was milled locally from their former mill. The sign was painted by someone for twenty-five dollars. Willie had been out putting up signs for a big circus that was in Houston.

After it opened in 1902, the ownership of the building changed hands multiple times within the family. It survived the 1915 hurricane that made landfall on the Texas coast as a Category 4 hurricane with sustained winds

Wunsche Brothers, located at 103 Midway, is the oldest standing structure in Old Town Spring. Today, the building is fenced off after a fire ravaged part of the structure. Everyone who knew Wunsche Brothers is anxiously waiting for the new owners to get it opened again. The ghost of Uncle Charlie is said to haunt the place, especially room number 5 upstairs. *Author's collection.*

of 135 miles per hour at the coast. By the time it hit Old Town Spring, the winds were 80 miles per hour and had caused significant damage, including to crops and the train depot across the street.

The Wunsche family started leasing the building in 1916 to different purveyors until it was sold. In 1919, during Harris County's law of prohibition, a man by the name of Joe Tojan was operating the saloon. The Texas Rangers came in and destroyed every bottle and keg of alcohol, shooting them up. It was sad that the first saloon to open also became the last to close. During the Depression, Uncle Charlie was known to hand out bread to help feed the hungry who were riding the trains looking for work.

One of the most notable people to lease Wusche Brothers was Viola Burke. It was called Spring Café during that time. She leased the property in 1949 and stayed for more than thirty years before finally retiring. She served hamburgers that were formed by hand from ground beef acquired from a butcher whose shop just so happened to be across the street. For years, people would come and stand in line to eat the inch-thick burgers, even though it seemed the building was falling apart and would come down at any second. Many store owners would claim the town as it is today was built because of these burgers. Entrepreneurs saw the potential in those lines; slowly, a few opened stores to take care of the people waiting to eat.

In 1982, it was purchased and remodeled by Scott and Brenda Mitchell, who fell in love while spending time in the café. Soon after the remodel, buildings were being occupied and other properties were being remodeled into stores. People started spending the day shopping in Old Town Spring and would make this restaurant one of their main stops. Before it burned down, the menu was only one page long and included hand-cut fries, burgers and fried chicken so big it took up almost the entire plate. One estimate was that the restaurant sold approximately thirteen hundred burgers a week. It had an area for musicians to play; a multitude of country music singers, including Clint Black and Lyle Lovett, have played here. I am looking forward to the time when it will be repaired and back up and running.

The story of the haunting here is that Charlie Wunsche is said to have fallen in love with a young woman who didn't love him in return. Brokenhearted, he lived the rest of his life with the pain of being rejected until his death in 1935 in an upstairs spare room of the place. People did not know that he was depressed because he always acted very cordial and happy. He stopped by tables to ask if anyone needed anything. He was very adamant that everything be in its place and the rooms be clean for the guests. It's not just Charlie who haunts here, but also Dell and, some say, a little girl. I cannot find any information on her identity. There was an artist who stayed in Uncle Charlie's old room about a year after his death. One night, he dreamed about a man who looked upset. He had long white hair, a black hat and a matching suit and was leaning over a table. He stood up and started pacing back and forth. The dream ended here because the artist woke up. Unable to go back to sleep, he drew the man from his dreams. The next morning, he showed several people his sketch; they were shocked. They claimed he had drawn the spitting image of Uncle Charlie. The man in his dreams must have been Charlie's ghost.

If you talk to any of the former staff, they will all tell you tales of working there, including after hours. One former staff member told me a story in which she was so frightened because someone came into the bathroom—but nobody was there. She told me that she was spooked to the point that she couldn't help but run out. She never liked to be anywhere in the building alone. I have been told that the former staff gets touched

The side of Wunsche Brothers today, after a fire ravaged the building. *Author's collection.*

and that you can see full-bodied apparitions that people believe is Uncle Charlie, and that he plays around with them.

On some nights, you can still hear the footsteps and clanking noises Uncle Charlie makes at his saloon and hotel. You can hear him moving from room to room, going up and down the stairs or rocking in his chair. Some have seen him looking out of the windows or sitting on the upper porch. Staff members would rearrange furniture or equipment before closing, then Uncle Charlie would start acting up because he didn't like change of any kind. He would move things around, lock doors and knock over tables or chairs. Items would become lost, and workers thought he took them. But the items would turn up in unexplained places. Anytime remodeling or construction was going on, the activity would escalate. Coffee machines were said to start and stop on their own, nozzles for the soft drink dispensers would disappear and then reappear later, unlocked doors would feel as though they were being held by someone on the other side, chairs would rattle and move about and strange shadows would move in the hallway upstairs.

One sighting was by a former waitress named Ilona Langlinais in 1984. Ilona was carrying a fresh pot of coffee in the upstairs hallway when she noticed an older gentleman dressed in a dark suit and a hat sitting alone at a table off to the side. After walking over to the man, she asked, "Would you like a cup of hot coffee?" He promptly disappeared, with a chilling wind sweeping around her. Another staff member thought she saw him one night as she was walking to her car. She looked back at the building, and when she looked up to where the liquor room used to be on the second floor, she saw what looked like a shadowy figure of a man staring out the window at her. People would notice the chair upstairs rocking on its own. Jana Beck told me about an experience she had here:

> *The very first time I ate at the Wunsche Café, I was pregnant with Alex. Walking in there, it's a feeling of energy like you never felt in your life, it's almost like walking back in time. There weren't many people there as it was a late lunch and the first thing I had to do was go to the bathroom. I was the only one in the bathroom at the time. I never heard anyone else come in, but when I was going I kept getting the feeling that I was being watched. Then I heard the stall next to me open and slam shut, and that was it for me! I just wanted to get out of there and back into the main room. I quickly washed my hands, because the hair on the back of my neck was standing up and it felt like someone was breathing on me. When I got out of there, I sat down at the table, shaking. I was asked if I was OK and talked to the waiter about it. They just laughed and said, "Oh, you met the Wunsche ghost, who is Uncle Charlie; don't worry, the ghosts are harmless." Freaked me the hell out!*

Many of our cases involved the trigger of things changing. Moving furniture, remodeling and any changes can make a location become more active. One of the intake questions most paranormal groups ask before an investigation is, "Have you made any changes to the environment?" Many times, this is followed up by, "Why, yes, we have. Why do you ask?" We do not know what happens from a scientific point of view that stirs things up, but it certainly does. It will be interesting to see what happens with the activity here when they finally repair and remodel the building. I spoke with Lupe Martinez, who told me:

> *I've lived here in Spring for a few years now. Not that I am psychic or anything of the sort, but to say the least, to put it in simple terms, I can sense things at times. Let's say, for example, when I first moved in, there was an eerie vibe I sensed. Not that it was an alarming intuition. Once I*

This photo was taken standing behind Wunsche Brothers, looking east. These abandoned buildings need tender loving care to bring them back to life. *Author's collection.*

begin to get familiar with the area and immediate surroundings, I took the liberty of exploring the fascinating shops. This is where I could distinctly sense a funny feeling. The restaurant that burned down at the corner of Old Town Spring I believe was once owned by one of the founders of Old Town Spring, which certainly has a history.

I once went inside the restaurant to have peach cobbler and had a blast with the stories of encounters the hostesses had with such restless spirits. I was even shown an antique photo hanging on the wall of what I believe was a family pic.... The young lady distinctly pointed out the image of what looks like a ghost who looked like a female adolescent that was standing at the window when the photo was taken. Just the same, I knew a man who claimed to be a descendent of the founders of this Old Town Spring. There are burial plots and a cemetery right on I-45 and Cypresswood right by Taco Bell. This guy would tell me stories of when he lived three houses from the restaurant right by the railroad tracks. He'd say there was a male spirit that would sit at the kitchen table and have coffee. It became such a regular occurrence that the ghost would no longer startle him. What I find so intriguing is what's up with so many restless spirits. There has to be some logic to this phenomenon.

A group called Paranormal Roadtripp uploaded a video online taken from the side of the building. In it, you can see what looks like someone moving upstairs through a window after hours, when there were no people in the building. Houston Ghost Tours has uploaded videos showing them running ghost box sessions outside the building and capturing voices from the other side. People have uploaded images to Facebook that appear to show apparitions standing on the porch upstairs or looking through the windows.

TRAIN CROSSING

100 Main Street
Spring, TX 77373

The tracks of the Houston & Great Northern Railroad are responsible for bringing twelve hundred people to live in Old Town Spring by 1910. It became a boomtown because of all the business in the wake of the railroad and its roundhouse and fourteen track yards. In 1915, a Category 4 hurricane made landfall on the Texas coast with sustained winds of 135 miles per hour. It had a devastating effect on Spring, destroying the original train depot, which was located closer to Wunsche Brothers Café.

In 1921, a steam engine derailed close to the crossing, bringing a crowd to the spectacle. On October 19, 1974, a gasoline truck with eight thousand gallons of gasoline crossed the tracks in front of an oncoming train at the Caroline Street crossing. It caused the deaths of both train engineers in a violent explosion that led the train to run through the town with the gasoline truck on the front of it. It was stopped south of the town, and the fire was put out by the Spring Fire Department. On August 10, 2015, not far from the crossing by Wunche Brothers, thirteen cars derailed; there were no fatalities. On December 6, 2007, a van was hit by a train after going around the crossing in an attempt to beat the train. It got stuck on the tracks and was pushed two hundred feet from the tracks. There were three fatalities in the van. The victims were all in their mid-twenties. The driver was the only survivor.

The tracks and the depot area in Old Town Spring. *Author's collection.*

The haunting activity reported by many people in the area of the crossing could be from Puffabelly's Restaurant, which has a history with the old Lovelady Depot. However, the tracks themselves have their own history, including multiple deaths. One reported story is about a man who lives in Spring who reported to police that he saw eerie lights coming from the area of the tracks near Puffabelly's. At first, he thought it was an oncoming train, so he stopped his car. He said there was no sound and no train, just slow-moving lights. He felt a rush of cold air as a headless man in overalls approached him waving a lantern. He feared for his life and sped off to get away.

Others report that signal lights come on, but there is no train. Some can feel a rush of wind as if it is coming from a train passing, but there is nothing there. Sometimes, you can see lights or what looks like sparks. You can see what looks like people walking, but they are not solid and disappear. Jana Beck, a resident of Spring, told me, "I hate going over those train tracks, especially at night, because I've seen shadows, figures and orbs galore.... Those tracks are crazy with activity!"

Not far from this spot was the Spring railroad water tower, which was used to fill the steam engines. It was kept filled by the railroad from Spring

The train depot and the water tower in Old Town Spring. Photograph taken in the early 1900s, from a postcard. *Courtesy Spring Historical Museum.*

East side of the tracks north of Noble Street. Shown are the hospital and a hotel before they were torn down in the 1920s. Photograph taken in the early 1900s. *Courtesy Spring Historical Museum.*

Creek using a gasoline pump through a four-inch pipe that reportedly is still in the ground. A few photos are helpful in showing the general location of the water tower. Spring was used as the watering hole for cattle. They would unload cattle from the trains, put them in pens and let them be fed and watered before moving them to other towns and cities. Fun memories have been made with that water tank. Some residents were said to climb up and go skinny-dipping in it. There are also stories of people fishing in the open tank. Trout and catfish that were small enough could swim from Spring Creek up through the pipe and into the tank.

The triangle of tracks just north of Main Street was where the roundhouse was located, according to maps and surveys of the area. The geological survey has the drawing of the roundhouse on the map. The Wiley Smith survey has the word *roundhouse* in the same area as does the geological survey. Gus Bayer opened a mill that produced packing material in 1927 in this location after the roundhouse was moved to Houston.

PUFFABELLY'S

100 Main Street
Spring, TX 77373

Puffabelly's is an American-style restaurant that serves some really good burgers. Its name derives from a children's song titled "Down By the Station." The song includes the lyrics "Down by the station early in the morning, see the little puffabellies all in a row." In this railroad town, one would daily see these black steam engines, called puffabellies for their puffing of white smoke.

The original structure that was at this location included the town's original bank and burned down on December 6, 1917. The fire started in a barn owned by John Brady. He started to crank his car and there was an explosion. It is believed that a spark and gasoline stored in the barn started the blaze, which spread quickly. His barn, which housed a few pigs, his personal residence and a rental house were all destroyed. A neighbor's property that contained the Spring Post Office was also damaged. There was no fire department in Spring back then, so people would gather with buckets in lines from a water source to try to fight the fire in what was called a bucket brigade.

The bank was rebuilt in its current location. The new structure that went up is what we would call a modern-day strip mall. The new structure burned down again on another occasion. In 1970, a laundromat burned down in this location. The next building on this spot was an old depot. Spring's original

Puffabelly's old depot restaurant is located at 100 Main Street in Old Town Spring, next to the railroad tracks. The ghost of a headless switchman came here not long after the Lovelady Building was occupied. Mysterious lights and phantom trains are said to pass by, perhaps caused by the deaths and fires that happened here. *Author's collection.*

depot, located closer to Wunsche Brothers, was destroyed for liability reasons after being damaged by the 1915 hurricane. The people believed the town needed an old railroad depot like the one that used to be in Old Town Spring again. The old Lovelady, Texas railroad depot came to the rescue. The building was the original depot in Lovelady that had been built in 1902. Lovelady is approximately two hours northeast of Spring. It just so happens that it is not only on the same railroad line as the original depot in Spring, but it was also built by the same man!

The building was purchased, disassembled and moved to Old Town Spring in the late 1980s. It then sat vacant for a time. Puffabelly's Restaurant was opened in 1995 in the old depot. It operated for about five years before it burned to the ground in 1999. Today, there is nothing left of the old building. The owner said, "We were not able to save anything." The restaurant was very popular, so the owners began rebuilding just one week later and got it back up and running within four months. The spirit of the building remains because they were able to secure old building materials so that the new building would have the same features as the old one. The depot also resembles the old building.

People have told stories of an unfortunate headless switchman associated with the old depot. It has been reported many times to haunt the inside and outside of Puffabelly's. He also haunts both Lovelady and Old Town Spring. For years, people in Lovelady reported seeing apparitions near the terminal. Several stories are about a headless man waving a lantern and moving up and down the front of the station near the railroad tracks. The legend has it that he was looking for his head. In 1902, shortly after the depot was constructed in Lovelady, the switchman tried to flag down a train headed down the wrong tracks. He was running toward the oncoming train, waving a lantern and yelling frantically when he tripped and fell underneath the train. He was decapitated. His badly mangled body was taken inside the depot; the floor was soaked with his blood, which left a stain. The good people of Lovelady reported seeing strange sights near the terminal not long after the accident. They reported seeing a man running with his arms waving frantically, and they saw lights.

When the fire in 1999 engulfed Puffabelly's, destroying everything, the only place not scorched by fire was the spot where, according to lore, his body was placed. Since moving the depot to this location, even up to today the headless switchman has been seen waving his lantern not far from the

Old tin ceiling in Puffabelly's Restaurant. *Author's collection.*

train crossing. Lights have been reported coming from the east side of the building closest to the tracks. A man said he stopped at the crossing because he was expecting a train because he saw lights. But there was no train, only lights and a rush of air followed by what he claims was a headless person wearing overalls running behind that light, as though he was trying to catch it. The frightened man reported the incident to the police.

Such activity sounds like what we call residual energy. A mysterious mechanism takes an event and stores the sequence of actions that will be replayed when unknown conditions occur—much like recording music to a CD or a movie to a DVD. Then a player can be used to bring the recording back from the past. In a haunting, unknown conditions cause the event to be replayed. Much of the activity here seems to be residual. It doesn't interact with anyone.

ZWINK HOUSE

100 Main Street
Spring, TX 77373

In the early 1870s, Jost Wunderlich bought one hundred acres of land on the west side of Kuykendahl Road and built a house. It was between Spring-Cypress and Rhodes Roads. Today, the Bridgestone West subdivision is on this land. This historic farmhouse was originally renovated by Mr. and Mrs. David Kleb and located not far off of Stuebner-Airline, approximately four miles from Puffabelly's Restaurant. The owners of Puffabelly's brought the building onto their property and started doing restoration. It was damaged in the fire that destroyed Puffabelly's. Local lore has it that at least one murder occurred in the house before it was moved to Old Town Spring. They say a man went out for a night on the town, drinking, and when he returned home, his wife was waiting for him on the porch. He had been told that she was having an affair earlier that night. He went in the house and got a shotgun, came outside and shot her dead. They say he went back into the house and committed suicide.

Peter Haviland Acch with Lone Star Spirits investigated the property at least four times with permission from the owners. They told me that, on one investigation, there was a shadow on the second floor that was watching them when they were discussing the case. They caught some anomalies in photos taken with an infrared camera, including what they believed was a mist. They also caught audio in the form of what we call an EVP, or electronic

Directly behind Thad's (shown here) is the Zwink House. *Author's collection.*

voice phenomenon, which sounded like a whistle. Pete then brought in a good friend, Lorraine Ross, who was a great medium, to do a reading on the house. She detected more than one death: one, a child from a snakebite; the other, a college student having an illicit affair with the owner's wife. She gave other details about the house's history that have been confirmed by the man who relocated the house. Someone told me that they believed house had been moved to another property, but it seems that it is still here.

In the area behind Puffabelly's there stands a small building that some say is the Zwink building. The local lore is that this building was an icehouse where, in the 1800s, bodies were kept on ice until there was room at the funeral home or were ready for burial. There was an icehouse not far from this spot in the triangle of the railroad crossings. It was used to keep things on ice before being sent by rail. The small building that stands here today was a former public restroom for the shopping area of Old Town Spring. They say it has repeatedly caught on fire. There is a sense of negativity around this part of the property. One claim is that insects are quiet here, as though it's a dead zone.

The curse of Old Town Spring is one reason people give for all of the fires that happen. The legend is that when the settlers moved into the area, the Akokisas or Orcoquisa Indians cursed the land. If anyone cut down a

Burned building behind Puffabelly's at 100 Main Street. It is sometimes referred to as the Zwinks, or the icehouse. Standing in this area for a long time, one notices that there is hardly any sound, including bugs. *Author's collection.*

tree or built anything on the land, they would experience a fire. Many of the buildings have been brought in from the outside and are believed to not be a part of the curse. By the 1850s, most of the Akokisas had merged with other tribes or died from European diseases to which they had no immunity, and they were angry. In the early 1800s, there were about thirty-five hundred Orcoquisa Indians within the counties that surround Houston, and there was a large village located not far from Jones Park on Spring Creek. Jesse H. Jones Park & Nature Center has re-created the Indian village, so you can see how they used to live.

Masonic Lodge

26514 Preston Avenue
Spring, TX 77373

Lodge no. 1174 was chartered on December 9, 1921. The original building was located on the corner of Preston and Gentry and had the address of 119 Gentry Street. Meetings in the two-story building were conducted upstairs in what used to be a cannery during World War II. The lodge operated out of this location for twenty-seven years before moving to a two-story building at 26304 Aldine-Westfield. Harris County Appraisal District shows that at its current location it was built in 1947 and is 3,870 square feet. It was donated on October 16, 1952, by member Gus Bayer.

It is said that the spirit of an unknown man looks out of the second window from the back on the right side of the building. Sometimes, while

The Masonic Lodge is located at 26514 Preston Street. If you stand along the side the building where the gravel road is, you can sometimes feel rain, even when no clouds are around. Some people think of the "rain" as ectoplasm. If you stand here, you may see a man peeking playfully out of the window. *Author's collection.*

Once a horse and wagon were the only way for a farmer to get to market. Today, the road to market from Spring is only about twenty-one miles and takes perhaps thirty minutes, depending on traffic. Back then, a journey took one day down to Houston and then one day back. Photograph taken in the early 1900s, from a postcard. *Courtesy Spring Historical Museum.*

you are walking by or standing in the gravel road next to the property, it feels as if it is sprinkling, even when no clouds are present. In this phenomenon, water mysteriously appears like rain. It is thought that these are spirits trying to get your attention. It's thought they condense the humidity in the air by their cold presence. Some believe it may be the tears of spirits of the Orcoquisa Indians who cursed the area when the steelers moved in.

Another, similar phenomenon is that of the sensation of walking through what feels like a spider web, but nothing is there. It can leave a wet substance on you. This moisture is thought to be what they call ectoplasm. Most of these sensations are dry experiences, however. It is believed that this is what it feels like if you walk through a spirit or if they walk through you. It is even more convincing when the temperature drops and we are able to up pick up a change in the readings in the electromagnetic field.

Noble Street Tattoo Parlour

26515 Preston Avenue
Spring, TX 77373

This is an Old Town Spring original home, built in 1906. One story states that it housed people from the lumber mill. This building just underwent a remodel to become Noble Street Tattoo Parlour. The work on the building began on January 17, 2017, by the current owner, Tommy Phillips. He spent every night until 3:00 a.m. working on the remodel with nothing weird happening. Then, on the night of the grand opening, February 4, 2017, something weird happened. There was a big party that included a keg and drinking. At about 11:00 p.m., people at the party could not get the bathroom door open. With ten people as witnesses in the room and concerned that someone had drank too much, had passed out or was hurt, Tommy kicked in the door to help whoever was in trouble, but nobody was in there. "The lock is a latch on the inside that would have needed someone to deliberately put it in there. It was freaky as hell. I tried to reproduce how if it was flipped up it could have locked itself but I couldn't get it to lock. I'm not saying it was anything but it was weird."

Paul and Sandra Van Fleet were the owners of the building when it was called Teacher Creature Store. They have moved to a new location in Old Town Spring. They told me that nothing much out of the ordinary happened while they were in this location. "Creepy but it's pretty quiet. There is a second floor; it is closed off, though. Travis has owned the building for

Noble Street Tattoo Parlor, located at 26515 Preston Street. An old tree stump taken out by the former owner has been said to be the hanging tree. Photos from the area where the tree was located show interesting anomalies. *Author's collection.*

Spring train depot showing the water tower by Noble Street at Hardey. Photograph taken in the early 1900s, from a postcard. *Courtesy Spring Historical Museum.*

twenty-three years and did not have anything happen out of the ordinary. He says the only thing was the rumor they hung someone from the tree. The tree is long gone, we took out the stump."

One thing we have noticed over the years of ghost hunting is that if a house had a closed-off area, it somehow contributed to the activity. In one house, the homeowner had put a padlock on the door to prevent anyone from going in or coming out. The house next door started to be demolished, and that's when all hell broke loose with activity. It started with what they thought were animal noises coming from the room; the sounds escalated. My suggestion to anyone living in a home with strange activity is to not lock away entire sections. Open them up to try to stop the activity.

Closest to the fire station to the left of Noble Street Tattoo Parlour was an old tree that several psychics claim is the hanging tree for the town. I have been told by several historians that there was no hanging tree here. Criminals were held in a caboose and shipped to Houston for trial and sentencing. There is also a story about a young boy who was playing around and accidentally hanged himself from one of these trees. I have not found anything to confirm a hanging anywhere in Old Town Spring, but it's interesting that anomalies in the trees have been seen by people.

Spring Fire Station

26511 Preston Street
Spring, TX 77373

I have heard that some say there is a curse on the land of the town, that we were not meant to occupy the land—so, when something is built here, it will catch fire. Much of the town was built with wood, not bricks. And the buildings are old. I interviewed several firefighters and found out that station no. 78 received many false alarms about fires before it stopped being an active station. There had even been false alarms that the station itself was on fire. The men at the station would get an alarm indicating a fire at the station where they were, but no fire would be present. Was this a phantom fire? The only death of a local firefighter happened inside the old town of Spring. The building on Preston Street is now being used for storage. Construction on the new station started in 2013 and was finally completed in May 2015. It is located on Louetta Road, close to I-45.

As you look at the right side of the driveway of the station on Preston Street, there is a tree that has some branches that hang over the driveway. Some say this is the hanging tree. Photos taken in this area sometimes show what looks like someone hanging in the tree. I could not find anything in old newspapers about any hanging in Old Town Spring. I also searched the story of an accidental hanging of a boy inside Old Town Spring and found no information. I met a woman named Angela Riel when I was going around talking to people about their experiences in Old Town Spring. She told me:

The roundhouse in Spring was located in the triangle where the lines meet. Photograph taken in 1902, from a postcard. *Courtesy Spring Historical Museum.*

I was taking a ghost tour through Old Town Spring and as I got closer to this one tree I started losing my breath. The tour guide stopped at the tree and explained it was a tree used to hang people. Could have been a coincidence. But I'm a tad bit of an empath so if someone in our group was getting short-winded, that could have also been it. But the feeling passed when we left the tree and never came back for the rest of the tour, not even after the group climbed up several sets of stairs.

Simply Texas

219 Main Street
Spring, TX 77373

Simply Texas, owned by Matthew Potter, is the current business at this address at the time of this writing. It manufactures and sells hot sauce. The building is known historically as the Bradley Home and is one of developer R.I. Robinson's very first houses in Old Town Spring. The property became famous during the time it was known as Rosie's Patio Café, known for the homemade bread the owner made fresh every day. A haunted rocking chair in the café was not on runners, but it would all of a sudden rock by itself. A friend of the owner named Luther was reported to have passed away from natural causes while in that chair. It also had an old iron that would suddenly fly off the refrigerator without hitting anyone and people would get locked out of the building. The keyless deadbolt would lock and unlock itself. The front door was reported to open and close on its own.

The former owner said that, one time, she walked into the room and saw the spring-loaded chair completely tilted back, as if someone unseen was sitting in it. It was as if they had leaned as far back as they possibly could. Then she saw the chair spring forward rapidly. It was as if someone had stood up, like a gentleman would do when a lady entered the room. I know many people who went there just to watch that chair. Before she moved out of the building, the rocking chair was pushed against a wall. She wanted to

Simply Texas is located at 291 Main Street. It is the former location of Rosie's Patio Café, which has been written about in several books on famous hauntings. A spirit here throws things around and likes to play with the locks. *Author's collection.*

prevent it from rocking and causing shoppers to become so frightened that they would run out of the store.

Lone Star Spirits came out to investigate the building one day. They secured the building and set up an unmanned camera inside the store to see if it could catch any activity. They caught a piece of paper falling on its own from the table to the floor, as if a breeze lifted it up by someone walking by really fast. They also caught audio of the deadbolt from the front door locking and unlocking itself several times. Pete Haviland said that the old lock needed grease and that it took effort to actuate it.

The current owner, Matthew, has experienced bottles thrown around and broken several times. Things will be moved around. In the bathroom, the lights go on and off by themselves. A shelf was taken off its pins and was leaning. One day, there were several people inside and it was raining; a woman walked in and didn't say anything, then disappeared. Matthew said that, even with the activity, he has never had any bad vibes in the building. He used to play with a friend in the Jefferson Davis Hospital (now Elder Street Artist Lofts). Matthew also told me that he doesn't like going in there. He gets very bad vibes there, as do many people. It was built on top of a

Inside Simply Texas, bottles are found thrown around without an explanation when employees open the store for business in the morning. *Author's collection.*

cemetery that includes victims of the yellow fever epidemic, Confederate soldiers and slaves.

Bill Curd, who lives nearby, told me that one day after his family relocated to Spring, they were spending time walking around and shopping in Old Town Spring. He said:

> *I was with my wife and daughters (they were in town) and we walked into Taste of Texas. I stayed in the front section while the rest walked thru the store. Whammo! A female spirit walked right thru me, and as she did, she whispered my name. I knew what it was and I sensed her there before she walked thru me. I do enough work as a medium to know what was coming. That's why I stayed there in the front of the store. She was gentle, it was a very loving connection, almost as if she knew me in another life. I have not done any past life work, so I'm not sure where I've been before. After she'd gone thru me and I had a chance to recover a little bit, I asked the girl at the counter who the lady is that just walked thru me. She absolutely knew what I was talking about and pointed me to the big corner white house where the medium lady hangs out on the porch. I asked her to show me the picture of the lady who hangs out there and even she knew I had just had communication. I didn't get an image of her, she went thru me too fast, but when the lady showed me the picture on the wall, I knew it was her, she let me know as I looked at the picture. I enjoyed the encounter because so many times when I remote view a client's home, I'm usually facing a non-friendly humanoid, or non-humanoid entity. I've been pushed, punched in the nose, had an entity get right into my face and yell at me to leave. I even did a remote viewing of the Black Hope Horror home here in Houston and was bum-rushed by an old spirit, but this woman walking thru me was pure gentleness, sweet, comforting.*

SOCIAL KNITWORK

26511 Keith Street
Spring, TX 77373

This business is aimed at the knitting and crocheting enthusiast. It sells a variety of yarns and needles. You can take a class to learn to knit, crochet, tat or spin. When I first moved to Spring, one of the business owners who knew I had a paranormal team wanted to take me on a personal tour of the town and show what she knew. One of those stops was this location, when it was empty and on the market for sale or lease. She told me about the fairies that lived in the trees. One tree is female and the other is male. They speak to each other through their roots and help each other to help the fairies that live here. The trees protect them. The male tree's job is to be the protector of the whole area, especially the female tree. The female tree's job is to nurture the fairies. She wanted me to put my hands on the trees and feel their energy. It is an interesting location, to say the least. Pictures that are taken at different times show different anomalies with different colors.

Another time we were going through the area on a ghost tour and I made a comment about the story of the trees. I was told that, yes, they knew about them and added that the tree that is farthest back by the fence is also a shape-shifter. If you take pictures of the tree, you can see a little girl swinging.

Across the street is a two-story blue building. If you stand and watch, you can see a black blob that moves around on the upstairs porch and comes

The Social Knitwork is located at 26511 Keith Street. The trees in the backyard are of particular interest to sensitive people. Fairies are said to live here, and one of the trees farther back on the property is said to be a shape-shifter. *Author's collection.*

down the stairs. It also moves like it is crossing its legs. A lady used to rent the space upstairs. She taught violin lessons. She talked about seeing the fairies across the street.

In addition to many shadows or dark blobs around Old Town Spring, there are also stories of lights. The paranormal is not just about the study of ghosts, but also of cryptids like bigfoot and UFOs. One of the shop owners told me about seeing lights over Preservation Park. Her son took video of the lights to show his mom so that they could figure out what they were. I have had several other people tell me about mysterious lights in the area. Bill Curd said:

> *Is anybody going to admit to this, am I the only one or am I nuts? I went outside last night to watch the meteor shower, but I got something completely different. I got to watch a bunch of white orbs or large globes chasing each other in one cloud—only one cloud. They were just chasing each other and when they got to the edge of the cloud, they turned around really fast and chased each other to the other side of the cloud. As the cloud moved, they moved and stayed in that one cloud. And, no, I was not drunk. So, I*

want to know if anyone else saw this. I'm going back outside tonight to watch more of the meteor shower and I hope I see it again, because it was amazing—totally amazing.

On April 4, 2015, several people uploaded to social media cellphone videos of lights from different locations around Old Town Spring. The lights were not planes or drones, according to the accounts of eyewitnesses. There have been a multitude of instances of people claiming to see lights all over Spring. Just outside of town, not far away, another person posted: "Did anyone else see the strange flashing lights behind Smith Elementary, the Pundt park is behind it. Right above the trees there. I took a video but it won't let me post it here."

What made Old Town Spring this hotbed of paranormal activity, with all the lights in the sky, dark blobs moving around town and sightings of ghosts? Is it all just coincidence? Perhaps a scientific explanation will be discovered one day. Perhaps the whole area is in a magnetic field. There are people studying different reasons for what could cause a person to see things.

Canadian neuroscientist Michael Persinger had been studying the effects of electromagnetic fields on the perceptions people have of seeing an apparition or sensing a presence. He believes that pulsed magnetic fields, which are imperceptible on a conscious level, can make you feel as if someone is in the room with you. The study created unusual activity in the temporal lobe of the brain. He created a device he called the God Helmet that created a weak magnetic field. After fifteen to thirty minutes, his subjects felt like someone was in the room with them. Many of the environments we investigate have magnetic fields that are picked up using EMF meters.

WHITEHALL

303 Main Street
Spring, TX 77373

One of the few original homes in Old Town Spring, this two-story, twenty-five-room Victorian home, called Whitehall, was built in 1895 by the Mintz family for $300. The sign in front of the house says the home was made of lumber from the heart of the tree: "Bell Bottom House." It was yellow and trimmed in white. It has changed over the years. In the 1920s and '30s, the Klein family lived here. They owned Klein Funeral Home and Klein Grocery in Tomball. After the funeral home burned down, they decided to turn the first floor of their residence into a funeral parlor. The downstairs room in the back of the property is said to have been the embalming room.

The home changed hands several times over the years. You can read about the changes outside the home, where a sign reads:

History
Built in 1895
1900s Mrs. McGowan's Boarding House
1920s Klein Resident—Klein & Tomball TX
1930s Funeral Home
1940s Converted into apartments WWII—photo Mintz Family
1950s Church & school house
1960s Hippie commune
1970s Commercial offices

Whitehall, also known as the Harper-Klein Home, is located at 303 Main Street. The spirits of a couple that died in 1933 are said to live here. Sometimes, they are seen on the upper porch, swinging. *Author's collection.*

The sign outside also includes a note from the owners: "This house was never grand—just a simple and well-constructed building with one secret room, but tells no secrets. I see my home as a kind forgiving old lady—gone through many changes, tough times, stood tall and very proud."

In this large house, there is rumored to be a secret room where two spirits keep to themselves unless the weather is warm and breezy. Behind the home is a dove cage; the birds coo when a spirt is around. For more than thirty years, it was reported that more than two hundred bats lived in a small colony within the attic of the house. Bats can be seen leaving right after dusk to go out in search of insects.

In 1933, a couple who was courting got into an accident on Riley Fuzzel Road, right where the road crosses Spring Creek. The young man drove off the bridge. The couple was killed after the car hit the bottom of the ravine. The next day, a local hiker came upon the car and the two bodies. The dead bodies were then taken to Whitehall, which was serving at that time as a funeral parlor for the town. A wake for the couple brought out a large crowd, grieving for the loss of two young people. Some say that if

The dove cage behind Whitehall, which was used as a sign to tell people when a spirit was around, indicated by the doves cooing. *Author's collection*.

you die young, you don't want to leave this world because you have so much unfinished business. Perhaps that's why they stuck around. Local lore says that the couple returned here, but it's probable that they never left. At some point, the couple became known as the Courting Ghosts of Whitehall.

Activity at Whitehall includes strange noises coming from upstairs, things being moved and full-body apparitions of the couple swinging on the porch upstairs. Randy Woods, former owner of the local paper, claims that their spirits are in a room upstairs. There is a pecan tree in the back of the property where three boys in the 1940s decided to build a treehouse. The young ghost couple would scare the boys away by making noises and shaking their treehouse. You can see remnants of the old treehouse and a sign made by the boys listing the original members of the kids' club.

Spirit Quest is currently located in this historic building. It hosts one of the ghost tours. I was shown a large black-and-white picture hanging on a wall downstairs of the home with some family pictured on the porch of the house. One day, with only one person in the building running the shop, they heard a loud noise in the back. They went to look to see what had happened and found an object that appeared to have been thrown.

This building is now the home of Chris and Ginger Pennell, who own the Spirit Quest Center, a retail gift and crystal shop. They offer psychic readings, massages, reflexology, reiki and energy work. They also have classes, workshops and events, including psychic and holistic fairs. It is home to one of the ghost walks and hosts an event called Dinner with a Ghost, which is a fun event in which you get to eat dinner and do an investigation.

Sedona Joe's

311 Main Street
Spring, TX 77373

This art and framing shop is said to be an original building and is thought by many to be the Sellers property. However, the Sellers house was located over on Hardy Road, according to a historian. If you look at a photograph of the Sellers house, the building looks identical to Sedona Joe's, with the exception of the dormers, which have changed. In the photo, the house next door even looks like Whitehall before the Victorian accents were added.

Owners Scott and Bryan Melton told me that they have seen strange things happen in their building. Others have, as well. One of the art residents of this location is painter Shawn Olson.

> *Shawn has moved into this space. He was in this space before we were. This was actually space that was rented to different artists as a working studio. He was one of the ones who rented, and people would get up and leave in the middle of the night and leave him sitting there. There is a great story about one night when he was moving into the building one night with his wife, Jessica, who is a counselor at Lone Star Community College. He was on one side and Jessica was by the door. She was looking around and saw this little girl standing there and she was saying "Hello," then Shawn says "What?" and she says "Who's this little girl?" Then the little girl*

Sedona Joe's is an art and framing shop located at 311 Main Street in Old Town Spring. The spirit of a little girl likes to play in here. *Author's collection.*

> *was gone. An adult would struggle with the back door, so try to imagine a very young girl trying this same thing. She simply did not go out that way.*

The back door was locked. It is too hard to unlock because there are two deadbolt locks. You would have to unlock both of those locks, then lift up the heavy door and pull. There was no way that she got out that door, nor did she go past Jessica.

In another incident here, angels were hanging on their ceiling. You can still see the hooks in the ceiling today. One day, the owner and his mom observed the angel being pulled all the way to the point where the spring is completely pulled out straight; it won't go back now. It was held and then let go by something unseen. The angel shot across the room and lost one of her glass wings. They were never able to find the piece of glass that came out. They keep the broken angel in a basket for the little girl to play with, since she liked it and they believe it was her that was pulling it.

They have toys for the little girl in a basket under a table. Sometimes, she pulls them out and leaves them lying around. They don't know much about the little girl, other than that she is very young and loves to play. Several psychics have come in at different times and told the owners that they see a little girl there.

Left: Owners Scott and Bryan have a basket of toys for the little girl spirit that lives inside Sedona Joe's. Sometimes they come in to find that the toys have been played with. *Author's collection.*

Below: Sellers Saloon and Mercantile building was, according to historians, located on Hardy Road. The structure in this photograph looks just like Sedona Joe's, with Whitehall next to the building, before the Victorian embellishments were added. Photograph taken in the early 1900s. *Courtesy Spring Historical Museum.*

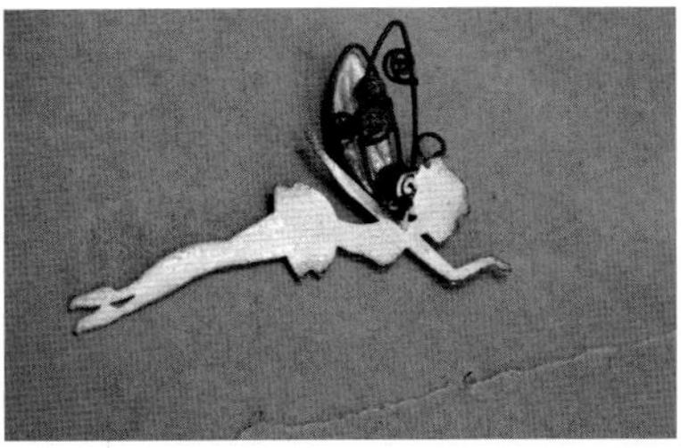

The broken fairy that was pulled back and basically launched across the room inside Sedona Joe's. You can see the glass missing from one of the wings that has never been found. *Author's collection.*

There is a dispute going on regarding how old the building is and how long it has been in this location if it had been moved here. The landlord told them he thought his family built it. Scott told me that the bricks were added. He said that if you look at the side, you can really see what looks like bricks over siding and that the siding is obviously not original. Where it's rotting at the bottom, you can see that it looks really old behind it. All of the wood in the attic looks creepy. Some of the wood is new, some old and some even burnt. So, the owners believe it's old. There was also no electricity or plumbing in the building, either.

While we were talking, the angel was accidentally dropped and the other wing broke. The owners said they thought that it would make her upset. They also said they believe that if you talk about her too much, she gets mad. Maybe the little girl was upset that we were talking about her and so she made it fall.

Houston Ghost Tours meets outside the building in the plaza to begin its Old Town Spring tours.

The Greater Church of Lucifer

310 Main Street
Spring, TX 77373

The Greater Church of Lucifer opened on October 31, 2015, and closed in 2016. When this controversial church opened in Old Town Spring, a spiritual tug-of-war began between those protesting outside and the people who had rented the building. Many saw this as a battle between good and evil. On one side, you had Christians and others who were mortified with a palpable anger and even hatred that people with these beliefs were moving into an area they loved. They believed the Luciferians were practicing devil worship. The protesters were in front of the building and across the street, praying, using bullhorns and saying things to anyone walking toward the building.

A few people said things like, "Satanists build altars and they sacrifice animals on altars. They sacrifice cats!" Others were letting people know "I have come here to let everyone know that Jesus is the answer and it's not Lucifer." Signs read "We reject Satan and his works." Others read "To love God is to hate evil." Tempers were flaring, and the police were called out to keep the crowd from getting out of control. Tape was put up outside the building to separate and protect everyone. Some of the protesters were filled with hatred towards what they believed was the devil operating around them. Several news stations filmed people protesting. One protester was yelling, "This is what we get with freedom of religion."

The Greater Church of Lucifer was located in the building at 310 Main Street. The spirit of a single male who died of natural causes is believed to be here, as well as that of a little girl, which mostly stays in the back part of the building. *Author's collection.*

Another protester said, "We are out here to inform the community that there is a Church of Satan in town. Anyone who has done the research on the subject knows that Satanists build altars and sacrifice animals on their altars as a form of worship to their god. That's dogs, cats, that's pigs and that's goats. It's a normal regular ritual to Satan."

Television and radio news stations covered the protests. People had come from all over, even as far away as Michigan, to stand around the building. One person said that her blood started to boil as soon as she heard the news that they were doing a grand opening of the devil in Old Town Spring. She believed, as did many others, that they were taking a stand against something that shouldn't be going on in the country or in anyone's community. They believed this church would have never come to be one hundred years ago. The protesters were trying to fill up the street so that anyone wanting to get to the building would have to go through the crowd. Harris County sheriff deputies escorted protesters away from the property. Some shop owners in Old Town Spring thought that the protesters were not giving the correct message: love everyone, even the Luciferians.

On the other side of this battle were the members of the Greater Church of Lucifer, who believed they were doing something great by opening up the church in Old Town Spring. They were trying to exercise their constitutional right to practice their religion. Co-president Michael Ford spoke about the church, saying that their church was not here to convert anyone. He said, "We don't sacrifice animals or worship the devil even though that's what everyone believes happens. We have gatherings but they are not services. We don't preach. They have the right to do what they are doing, but we have the right to believe in what we do, too, and we need to co-exist."

Luciferians believe that, with the fall of Lucifer from heaven, he was being set free from the chains of bondage. Lucifer is seen as an example of a free thinker. Luciferianism is closely related to Satanism, but there are some differences. Satanism represents the self and indulging in earthly pleasures. A person is his or her own God. Luciferians are more into personal, self-directed evolution that brings power and wisdom to the higher self. Christians interchange the names "Lucifer" and "Satan."

So much anger and frustration was building in this area of town. The protests went on and off until the Luciferians left. The building kept getting vandalized. The Luciferians received death threats; even their neighbor's shop received threats. This area of Old Town Spring has negative environmental energy from this long tug-of-war. Logan Corelli told me:

> *Atmospheric haunting from trauma, extreme emotions, anger, rage, sadness, severe depression, these things that can actually become contained within an environment or an object that was in the environment. We don't know exactly what creates the environmental energy to stay and cause a haunting. There are people who are sensitive to this energy when they come into contact with it. It effects people in different ways. One person may walk in and feel a sense of apprehension and fear, and another can feel cold. They can acknowledge the sensation differently. Some people can also interpret the energy as though they are seeing people. It doesn't always manifest in a physical way. As an example, let's say you are looking down the hall and you can see a man. That's one thing. But it is another thing if you get an impression of a man. Then it really is more of a psychic impression.*

I know people who won't come to Old Town Spring at night because they feel scared, especially after dark. My friend Richard Montes won't come to this area because he is afraid of the energy

> *To be honest I've been avoiding Old Town Spring at night for that reason. It's hard to explain but I've been stressed so I feel more accessible to negative energy. Like it feeds off of me. I've even been having problems in normal places. When I'm stressed or sad, "things" tend to follow me. I don't know how to explain it. Things are always in my peripheral, always behind me or in the shadows everywhere I go, and it is worse in places with activity. Like, my chest will get tight and my blood pressure will rise, with physical and measurable effects.*

This building, which is not original to Old Town Spring, is split into two commercial spaces. I was told that inside, the space the Luciferians occupied, which is in front, had negative energy here even before they moved in. This energy prevented one of the current Old Town Spring shopkeepers from renting the building. I know many people, however, who would rent a space because they believed it was haunted. Several colleagues of mine have rented spaces that were supposedly haunted specifically to conduct a study over time so that they could understand the activity within the building. These long-term projects have been valuable for us in learning about the paranormal. One of the special project locations is Logan County Memorial Hospital in Guthrie, Oklahoma. Logan Corelli wanted to share his experience here. "The biggest advantage to having a place like the hospital is that the number one thing is it is closed off to outsiders. Everything that goes on inside the building has no contamination from anyone. The other good thing is that you have a big area where possibly people died and you get multiple things that happen in there. Many things have happened to us in there over the years. It was the most convincing place that I have been to convince me that the paranormal is in fact real."

That research project started in 2001 and is still an ongoing study. The building has audio equipment and many cameras that are accessible online to view the activity. People from all over the world log on to observe and document anything they see. I encourage anyone interested in the paranormal to rent any building they think may be haunted to study it.

Patricia Rickard, a gifted medium, used to have space in the same duplex building as the Luciferians. She told me about the spirits in the building. A Hispanic man haunted the back part of the building and probably went all through it. He seems to be the most active spirit in this location. He was single when he passed away from natural causes. There is also a little girl who occupies the space. Both of these spirits have been confirmed to be in the back part of the building. "We will be sitting, especially at night, I will be there and I will hear somebody just walk down the hall and my front door is locked. You can feel it coming down the hall and there is nobody in the hall. It is kind of spooky sometimes."

Satanic worship is more about sacrificing to the devil rather than bringing in demons. Whether intentional or unintentional, it is possible that something was conjured or brought here through channeling. Something could have been summoned and then attached itself to the property.

Part of my intake as a case manager was to ask if the client had ever practiced alterative religions. Much of our caseload involved either alternative religion practice or conjuring of some kind through playing around with a dark art or a Ouija board. It's believed that the use of these objects can open doorways to another dimension, which people in the paranormal field call the other side.

Rebel Birth

315 Main Street
Spring, TX 77373

This building now belongs to Kathleen Wilson and Joli Ammons, who are both doulas. A doula is a woman who is trained to assist another woman during childbirth and who may provide support to the family after the baby is born. Rebel Birth offers support groups, parenting education and childbirth education. They say that, unlike James Dean, they are rebels with a cause. "We aren't here to ruffle feathers or put on a show. We are here to remind you that you are in control of your healthcare. To improve the establishment by putting the reins back into your hands! You don't have to choose between the red pill and the blue pill. You can choose the green pill, or even no pill!"

Kathleen told me they were excited when they moved into their building in July 2016, and nobody told them anything about spirits in their building. Her partner is very afraid of spirits and anything paranormal.

After they moved in, strange activity began to be noticed little by little. One interesting thing that happens has to do with the air conditioner. It gets turned off about once every week or two. It's completely shut down when Kathleen comes in to work. This activity also happens in my building, although less frequently. Rebel Birth is directly behind what used to be Cathy Nance Studios at 324 Gentry Street, which was my old building. Both of us have had the air turned off when we come in, but nobody is doing it. My

Rebel Birth is located at 315 Main Street and has the spirit of a little girl in it. The air-conditioning gets messed with, and a chair spins on its own. *Author's collection.*

air-conditioning unit used to stay on when plugged in. It's not digital, it has dials for controls that stay where you set them. If the electricity cuts off due to a power outage, my unit would come back on at the temperature at which I had set it.

There is a chair in the office that moves on its own. It had once belonged to Kathleen's father. It happens at random times when you are least expecting it. Imagine you are busy with your work and then you notice something that catches your attention out of the corner of your eye. It makes you turn to look, and there you see the chair turning, and nobody is doing it. The secretary also talks about how she sees a little girl with dark hair by the back door, out of her peripheral vision. She's only noticed her by the back door.

Many of the calls to Woodlands Paranormal come from people who work in the medical field. The theory is that, if someone works so closely with life and death, they somehow attract spirits who then follow them home. The little girl who is seen here may have already been here, or perhaps she followed one of the owners here and decided to stay.

The interior of Rebel Birth is filled with beautiful artwork from an artist they chose to feature. Their goal is to change out the art from time to time, not only to fill their shop with beauty but also to help an artist. It is a very comforting and nurturing environment, and this may be the reason that the little girl is here.

Black Sheep Bistro

326 Main Street
Spring, TX 77373

Maria Gagis Macri, the owner of Black Sheep Bistro, told me that when she first walked into the building she felt so completely at peace. She knew this space was for her, and she moved in. Every time she walks in, she feels the same sense of peace come over her. "I'm on the spiritual side to begin with. So, I feel great energy in the Black Sheep Bistro. I knew the building embraced me and Joe. We feel very loved when we walk in the doors."

One day, Sandy overheard a girl talking to her mom. Sandy told me, "I'm so hooked on Old Town Spring! I go back as often as I can to shop and hang around with the spirits. I can feel the energy of ghosts. Some places are filled with peace like this one and some places are sad. At lunch, I overheard a conversation where a little girl said, 'Mommy, the ghost scratched me.'"

Rowan Dark with After Dark Tours used to work out of this building at one time. She told me that you always just knew that someone was watching you. There were cold spots and also a smell that she couldn't describe but that she said was always present. There are other buildings around this one with activity, like the blue building with white trim behind it. Maybe it is all the same spirit going in and out of these few buildings. Maybe there is a sound—called infrasound—being generated in the area that is creating these feelings.

The Black Sheep Bistro is located at 326 Main Street. It has an energy or vibe that people pick up on in different ways. You should go visit, stay for a bite to eat and try to see how you feel in this location. *Author's collection.*

Sound at levels that humans can't hear can cause distinct physiological features. Infrasound is referred to as super low-frequency sound. It is sound that is lower in frequency than twenty hertz, which is the normal limit of human hearing. If the intensity is high enough, it is possible to feel the vibrations from infrasound in various parts of the body. Elephants and other animals use infrasound to communicate, in some cases over long distances. Infrasound can be produced mechanically and is also produced naturally through waterfalls, storms, winds, surf, weather patterns and earthquakes.

Scientists studying the effects of mechanical things that create low-frequency noise found in persons feelings of disorientation and panic, as well as changes in heart rate and blood pressure, which can make people feel as though they are being visited by a ghost. In the paper titled *The Ghost in the Machine* which was published in the Journal of the Society for Psychical Research in April 1998, Vic Tandy described working in a lab with a haunted room. Whenever Tandy worked here, he felt depressed and uncomfortable. He heard and saw things resembling a ghost. He discovered that the room had a fan that was operating at nineteen hertz, and he believed that inaudible vibrations were causing the haunting.

The Well

318 Main Street
Spring, TX 77373

Before Spring became a town, when it was forming as Camp Spring, there is said to have been a man who was a serial killer. It is said that he dumped bodies of children into an area well. The well at this location of 318 Main Street is sometimes indicated as the killer's well on ghost tours, but it is not in fact the actual site. The well here is a recent man-made water feature, not an actual well. People will say that when they are at this well, they feel a vibration if they lean against it. Is it all in their minds? It may be similar to the act of giving someone a placebo that evokes a real response. In this phenomenon, a sugar pill with no active ingredients is given to a patient. The patient believes it is a real pill; because their mind believes it is real, it can sometimes improve their condition. This happens simply because of the person's expectations. Tell someone a story of a place vibrating, and they may feel the vibration when they are there.

The location of the actual old well from the serial killer story is reported to be at 218 Noble Street, next to Thyme Square, under a house. That old house has been rebuilt in the last few years and has had a couple of other buildings added to the property. I recently moved my photography studio into the blue cottage and have already done an investigation. The night of that investigation, we had a psychic out with us who didn't know the story of this area and kept hearing the name Ella. We had meters going off for a bit,

The Well is part of the ghost tour circuit. There is an electromagnetic energy here that you can pick up on with an EMF meter. This is not the dumping site of a serial killer. *Author's collection.*

as well, seemingly related to questions we were asking. The light outside kept going on and off then flickering all night even though the bulb was screwed in. On another night, one of the town's residents showed the spot where the well was located to a group doing a ghost tour. Some people feel a sense of sadness, imposing doom while standing or walking through the area of this well. Inside the blue building, all I am feeling is happy—at least for now.

Going back to the 318 Main Street location, there are reports of spirits in this general area. Many of the cottages were brought here from all over. They all have their own energy and memories. The well trickles water all the time; the water splashes against the stones. Some believe this creates an energy field that theoretically is needed to help spirits manifest. One theory is that moving water creates a magnetic field, especially when running through limestone. If you run equipment around the well, it will sometimes pick up spikes in EMF (electromagnetic fields).

Geomagnetic fields (GMF) are direct current (DC) and are produced naturally by Earth. Some things can produce changes in the strength of the field, like seismic activity and electrical activity from thunderstorms. There has been a considerable amount of evidence gathered through studies over the years that suggests that changes in the field can have an impact on behavior. It produces things like sleep disturbances, mood shifts and anxiety. Some studies suggest that people who happen to have epilepsy, brain injuries and sensitive temporal lobes may be susceptible to changes in the activity in the field. Talk of higher fields have people reporting seeing apparitions.

Electromagnetic fields are alternating current (AC) and are produced by electricity running through homes, via cords that are plugged in, appliances and electrical boxes. It is also present in natural forms.

Prolonged exposure to these magnetic fields has sometimes caused people to experience what they perceive as a haunting. They will report apparitions, experiencing a presence and having the feeling of being touched. They also report having nightmares and being generally scared in their environment.

When our group, Woodlands Paranormal, goes out to investigate a case, we first check for high frequencies. We use Tri-Field Natural Meters and other gadgets to measure the EMF/GMF. When we detect a high field, we make suggestions to the homeowner or business owner, such as moving furniture out of a high-frequency zone, unplugging appliances or calling an electrician to check their wiring.

We investigated a case in which a homeowner reported being touched, her hair standing on end and seeing things move. As we were going from room to room, we found that our meter indicators moved as high as they could go around her bed in the master bedroom. We were able to follow this field to the back wall. Outside the house, against a wall, multiple wires were coming in from a box not far in the backyard. We were told by the homeowner that she had had an addition built, and that is part of where her bedroom was located. It looked like she hired an inexperienced electrician to wire the addition. We suggested that she not sleep in that space, as it was most likely causing her haunting, and to call an electrician as soon as she could. We found out that she followed our suggestions, and this stopped her haunting.

Chakra Shop and Tarot

400 Main Street
Spring, TX 77373

This metaphysical shop offers a host of readings, including medium and tarot. It also offers pet psychic readings, pet chakra balancing, crystal stone readings and chakra balancing. Some believe there is the spirit of a Native American living around here. Dee Adams, one of the owners, said that a lot opened up spiritually in Old Town Spring from the Indians losing their land. The story that started at the Envy Wine Room location with Dee picks up again here at this location, where Dee and Rachel Stevenson moved their business in May 2016.

On one hot day, as the new construction was going on, they were waiting for utilities to be turned on. The construction was noisy, and it was stifling inside. She decided to visit the museum across the street and walk around to get some cool air. As she was around the corner, behind the museum, she found the photograph of the woman who had been following her around.

Dee walked into the new store and felt a male energy. She was going to cleanse when she got in there, so she wasn't worried about it. She gave a key to her contractor, who is a good friend of the family. She went over to check on the progress he was making about a week after construction started. He was standing outside shaking his head at her and laughing. Then he told her that he was having the hardest time getting the stuff done where he could finish the project because he keeps getting locked out and his tools keep going missing.

Chakra Shop and Tarot at 400 Main Street. It is home to a spirit that likes to lock doors and move stuff around. *Author's collection.*

Dee and Rachel walked in the building, and the contractor's mother was there, painting in the corner. Dee asked how things were going, and the mother told her that she had told the contractor to get out of here because he was messing with all of the workers. About a week later, she passed away in her rocking chair.

Toward the end of life, many people talk about seeing folks around them that nobody else sees. Sometimes, it happens right before death; at other times, they talk about them for weeks. We had a case one time in which a mother was taking care of her son who had been diagnosed with cancer three years before he passed away. In the last six months before he died, he would say things related to people who weren't there. He would ask who the man was that his mother walked in the door with or if grandma could come sit with him again. He had conversations with people who weren't there. She was seeing shadows during that time and was scared. The shadows were still around her house, even though his death had occurred about eight months prior.

The theory is that there is a thinning of a veil, or a doorway is opened, toward the end of life, allowing those who are going to pass through to be comforted by those who have gone before. Maggie Callanan is a hospice nurse who has witnessed more than two thousand deaths over a twenty-

Old Spring gas station. Photograph taken in the early 1900s, from a postcard. *Courtesy Spring Historical Museum.*

seven-year career. Patients of hers have said they could see family members who had died. They told her that their loved ones were waiting for them; they had to get their bags together for a trip; they had someplace important to go; and they had to go home. Many skeptics say that these people were confused because of medication or the shutting down of neural pathways. Callanan, who coauthored a book, *Final Gifts: Understanding the Special Awareness, Needs, and Communications of the Dying*, believes such patients are getting a glimpse of life after death, which she believes exists. She says, "But frankly, the confusion is ours. The patient knows what's going on."

There is another interesting feature of this corner property. As you stand on the front porch of this store, you can look across the street and almost see the past. Look where the road splits in front of the historical museum and see the field where the sugar mill was located. Back when the area was young, nearly everyone in Old Town Spring had a sugar cane patch on their property. People from around the area would bring the cane stalks to the sugar mill for processing into syrup. The juice from sugar cane was pressed by wheels driven by horses or mules; it would then be boiled in a large cast-iron kettle to produce the syrup. Some believe that you can still see the happy spirits of people on their way to the mill.

Yours Truly

32½ Noble Street
Spring, TX 77373

This shop is a hip, plus-sized resale business. Mandy Holverson, who owns the store, understands how difficult it is for plus-sized women to find clothes. And she also understands the importance that the clothes be hip and affordable. She wants to make her clients feel good wearing them, and she knows people are willing to seek them out. Mandy told me that they have had activity in their building since they moved in.

> *We actually have had two experiences here at our store. My sister Jessie lived in our building for a few months so she might have some better stories. We often hear strange noises like footsteps, and the shop bells on the front door sometimes jingle wildly as if the door has been opened, when it has not been opened, and is even locked! As for me—one day I was working on painting a sandwich board sign for our shop by myself. My sister and I had made a mistake trying to use marker over the paint. I realized the marker never set or dried and that I could scrub it off. So, I decided to throw it in the tub and run the shower over it to keep from making a mess as I scrubbed. I had the shower head turned against the wall and it is kind of hard to move the shower head; honestly, it's cheap and old, so I felt pretty comfortable that it wasn't going to spray me. For a few minutes, everything was fine, then it literally turns completely towards me and is spraying me*

Yours Truly is located at $32\frac{1}{2}$ Noble Street and has its very own spirit. He actually turned and sprayed water at the shop owner, hitting her in the face. *Author's collection.*

> *in the face! I reached down and tried to shut it off, and the thing will not shut off. I ran out of the room to grab a towel, came back and tried again to shut off the water. Finally, it worked. My first thought was, "Thanks a lot, ghost!" Which I also said out loud. Followed with, "You know, that wasn't very nice, I don't want to be cleaning up water all day!" That experience would be weird enough except for what happened next. I returned to our kitchen, where I had all our paint supplies set out. I finally get everything prepared so I can lay down and finish painting the sign. Suddenly behind me I hear a loud crash and see that a gallon water jug has fallen off the top of the refrigerator, the cap is off and it's pouring water all over my laptop and countless paperwork on our mini kitchen table. That, of course, set me back another twenty minutes on my project cleaning up. I was fuming. I never really feel scared or malicious intent, but I do feel like our ghost likes mischief. Our house, like many in OTS, is not original to its land. It was shipped in from elsewhere with no way of knowing what stories, or spirits, it brought along the way!*

This is yet another example of an intelligent haunting. We believe a person after death may not pass into the light for various reasons, including free will. Perhaps they feel that they have unfinished business, like telling a loved one of an injustice done to them. Maybe they don't even realize they are no longer alive. Perhaps a car accident happened and they died in an instant. Sometimes, they cannot go into the light because they don't want to let go of the living. Others may fear the other side or judgment.

When a person passes away, they continue to have the same personality that they had while they were alive. Think of the movie *Ghost*. Sam was a nice guy who, after he passed away, continued to be a nice guy. He was hanging around trying to warn Molly about the danger she was in. If a person was mean while alive, they will continue to be mean after death. Many people think of negative activity as if it were a demon, but it can just be a bad person. Demonic activity has certain hallmark features that will differentiate it from a run-of-the-mill haunting.

The following are signs of an intelligent haunting. These events occur at different times of the day and have no discernible pattern of occurrence.

Objects disappear and reappear in impossible places over a period of time
Unexplained cold/hot spots
Strange and unexplained sounds or voices
Furniture and small objects are moved
Objects or furniture thrown
Doors, windows and cabinets opened, closed, slammed or unlocked/locked
Lights, televisions, radios and faucets turned on and off on their own
Unexplained smells or the feeling of being touched
Strong sense of a presence, including the feeling of being watched

Jailhouse Saloon

310 Preston Street
Spring, TX 77373

The jailhouse sat empty for thirty years before being renovated into what is now the Jailhouse Saloon, owned by Heidi Bothmann. The original jail in Old Town Spring was built behind Robinson's strip center on Main Street, where Puffabelly's is now. It was constructed of wood and burned down during the 1917 fire. For some time, the jail was located in a train caboose. Prisoners were taken once a week to jail in Houston. When the jail was rebuilt, the location was changed to Preston Street at the train crossing. The Jailhouse Saloon is the current occupant of the second building to house the jail, which also included a courthouse. That building was approximately twenty feet by twenty feet and constructed of wood. It was once again rebuilt using cinder blocks for the part of the jail that housed inmates. It is believed that the spirit of a man is here, throwing things around. We do not know who this fellow is, but he is defiantly there. Heidi said, "Oh, yeah, we do have one particular 'guest' of the Jailhouse! I don't know any particulars about this 'guest,' but two different mediums on two separate occasions have both given me the same name. We've had customers and bartenders who've had experiences, but nothing to me personally. I think this 'guest' likes to pick on people they don't like!"

People have had coolers thrown at them. Boxes stored up high have fallen on employees. Some items have been tossed or have fallen next to

Jailhouse Saloon on Preston Street by the trail crossing. The jail is in the brown building on the front left side. There is a special guest here who tosses things at people he doesn't care for. You should spend some time at the saloon and see if the ghost throws anything at you. *Author's collection.*

them. This is yet another spirit in Old Town Spring that tosses things around. It is speculated that this man might have been in jail here for a time. He seems to lose his temper and lash out at certain people. We don't know who he is, but it sounds as though he is engaged in what we call an intelligent type of haunting.

One night, Woodlands Paranormal conducted an investigation with the owner. We got audio responses from what we believe is a male spirit. We were almost having a back-and-forth conversation, asking it questions and getting responses that we could clearly understand. Mitch Martino had been conducting new audio experiments; we have been getting amazing results using these new methods. The male spirit here clearly liked a former waitress who had recently left. In addition, one of our female team members was scratched while investigating. A photograph of a handprint was made using a FLIR (forward looking infrared) camera.

Many old jails are known to have paranormal activity. The theory behind all these hauntings is that the high emotions that come from being imprisoned get imprinted by some mechanism onto the building. This imprint or energy is believed to cause a residual haunting, in which the activity that is seen is repeated without any interaction with the living. The high emotional energy can also attract spirits.

The jail is a place of physical suffering, lacking creature comforts. Its occupants fear long sentences, losing their rights and losing hope. Jail is an emotional rollercoaster. Inmates may plot revenge against those who snitched on them. Some spirits may linger here because they aren't aware that they have passed away; they still believe they are in jail.

Thyme Square

200 Noble Street
Spring, TX 77373

There was a Civil War museum at this location, housing numerous artifacts. The museum also hosted Civil War reenactments, and the Eleventh Texas Calvary made its home here. Apparitions of Civil War soldiers have been known to appear among the actors when they held battle reenactments. Lone Star Spirits with Pete Haviland investigated the area and looked at footage of one of the reenactments and discovered a glowing ball of light on the film. It was interesting that the photographer was told where to point his camera before he took the photo. She saw a disfigured soldier from the Civil War standing in the middle of the square.

Perhaps some of these apparitions were attached to artifacts or articles of clothing. Woodlands Paranormal has seen multiple cases in which an object has such an attachment. One such case involved a family that was terrified after seeing things move in their house. They also had the feeling of being watched. On this investigation, we found that the homeowner's father's military uniform, which was hanging in the back of a closet, was producing EMF. We were able to use tools to take readings. This was one factor that made us believe her father was attached to the uniform and was thus hanging around her home. The family stopped being scared when they had an idea of what was there.

Old Town Spring Meat Market. You can see "Meals 25 cents" hanging on an old sign. Photograph taken in the early 1900s, from a postcard. *Courtesy Spring Historical Museum.*

EMF is a type of energy that we can measure. We can show that energy is present in some form. To give you an idea, EMF is found everywhere that electricity is in use, around any object that has an electric charge. It is an invisible force that surrounds electrical devices and wiring with an electric current running through it. The refrigerator in your house is one of the biggest producers of EMF. It is not healthy to spend considerable time inside an electromagnetic field.

Another haunting case with attachment to an object involved paranormal researcher Todd Dreher. He wanted to share information about this case as a warning to those who seek out estate sales for interesting things to buy.

> *Be careful of estate sales. I was called out three years ago to help in a case where a man's wife was being attacked. They couldn't figure out why only the wife was being attacked. We got there two days after one bad attack happened, and there were scratches still all over her back. She had a bruise on her cheek, as well. As we were there, we were standing by each other with the wife, who had a baseball cap on and a ponytail. We watched her ponytail stick straight out, and in seconds, her head yanked*

back so hard and fast she fell backwards. Two of us caught her before she hit the floor.

I finally asked the right questions and found out the husband had bought a set of wedding rings in an estate sale. He had them in the house but hadn't given them to her yet. The husband and wife had gone to New York and, two days later, their son was calling them, telling them something was going on, because the pictures in the hallway of his house were turned sideways, upside down and even on the stairs. The parents thought he had bumped them or something. This went on for two more days, and they could tell he was scared as hell about something. They finally went home and had no clue what was going on.

As soon as he gave his wife the rings, within an hour things were happening to her. After being punched in the face, they called my friend with another paranormal group. They thought they had a poltergeist. That's when they called me, because I had an experience with one before.

They went on this case, investigated and couldn't figure out why only the wife was being attacked. Through their investigation, they found out that the original owner of the rings had passed away. Her husband loved his wife so much that he had kept her rings. They were not sure if the man had them custom-made for his wife or if he just purchased them from a jeweler. When he passed away, for whatever reason he continued to stay attached to the rings. Todd says, "That explains why she was the only one getting attacked. He was telling the woman, "Take those off because those are my wife's." I told them we need to do a cleansing now, which we did. It's been clean since and no more problems."

PART II

DRIVE AROUND OLD TOWN SPRING

Spring Cemetery

26206 Aldine Westfield Road
Spring, TX 77373

This site was designated as a Texas Historic Landmark in 2001, before even Old Town Spring was designated a landmark. The marker reads:

> *After Spring was established on the International and Great Northern line in 1873, it became an important railroad center. The Sellers family, early area landowners, donated a portion of their property for a community church and cemetery. The oldest legible tombstone is that of a child, Franklin Leroy Lovins, who died in 1910. Military veterans including George C. Baker, who served in the Civil War, are also interred here. Gravestones mark nearly 50 burial sites, but many other burials are unmarked. The cemetery stands as a reminder of Spring's heritage as a railroad town.*

In the fall of 1999, Harris College honors students took on the restoration of the cemetery as part of a community service project. They were able to find and mark the headstones of approximately fifty grave sites, and there are many other burials that are unmarked. After the town was settled, the residents needed a place to lay their loved ones to rest. The Sellers family, early area landowners, donated a portion of their property for a cemetery

Spring Cemetery behind the church on Aldine Westfield Road has fifty burial sites. One important grave is that of George C. Baker, who served in the Civil War. *Author's collection.*

Members of Woodlands Paranormal investigating the cemetery. You can see an anomaly by the couple standing to the right. In an enlargement of the image, the anomaly resembles an animal of some type. We did not see an animal or anything unusual at the time the photo was taken. Looking at consecutive photos taken that night reveals this as the only image with orbs in it. *Author's collection.*

and a church. The cemetery is located just outside Old Town Spring on Aldine Westfield.

This cemetery is a part of several ghost tours and has been investigated by multiple teams. EVPs have been caught, and anomalies have been seen in photographs taken at this site.

Bayer Lumber Yard

26718 Aldine Westfield Road
Spring, TX 77373

When Spring started to grow, a strong demand for lumber began. The very first mill was off Spring School Road in what would later become the opera house. Of all the mills, Bayer became the most important. The first mill that Gus Bayer opened, in 1927, was located where the roundhouse used to be, inside the triangle to the north of the railroad crossing at Main Street. The Excelsior Mill produced packing materials made from wood and leaves. He then built a sawmill right next door to the first one. Finally, he built his largest mill on Aldine Westfield Road. There were several fires over the years, with the worst engulfing most of the mill in 1954. In June 2011, there was another fire, which spread to several structures. Arthur Edward Bayer, son of Gus Bayer Jr., continued to work out of the office until his death at ninety-two on Saturday, September 17, 2011.

A man who used to live close to Bayer Lumber saw a photo that someone had posted of the office building. He talked about his memory as a child hanging out with his dad and Mr. Bayer: "I grew up on the property right behind Bayer Lumber. We used Bayer Water Company, as well. I moved away thirty-two years ago, and it didn't look much better back in '79, but as a kid, it was always fun going in there with my dad. Arthur Bayer would be sitting on a stool behind the counter smoking the biggest, smelliest cigar you

What is left of Bayer Lumber Company today on Aldine Westfield Road. Most of the brush and overgrowth has been removed. *Author's collection.*

Old sawmill and lumber yard. Photograph taken in the early 1900s. *Courtesy Spring Historical Museum.*

could imagine. As soon as I saw that picture, I could smell that cigar and see Mr. Bayer and my dad shooting the breeze."

Over the years, I have talked to people who have said they saw things at night as they drove down Aldine Westfield, passing the Bayer home and the lumber yard. Before construction widened the road, one-hundred-year-old oak trees covered in Spanish moss draped across part of the road. It always looked creepy. The old mill looked abandoned and overgrown. There are tales of typical accidents from moving lumber and working with saws. It's good that the hospital was located about one block away, on Hardey Road. Audio caught in the area is said to sometimes catch electronic voice phenomena of a whistle, like the one blown at the sawmill. Today, the trees are gone, as is the brush at the yard. You can still see some old equipment at the site, like a giant wheel.

Bayer Home

26623 Aldine Westfield Road
Spring, TX 77373

Rachel Walker O'Neil's grandfather owns this big house, which is a landmark in the area. I was told that behind the house on the same property is a gray house that a doctor had once lived in and had committed suicide there. The residents believe he is still haunting the house. All the cousins would get together and spend the night, and scary things would happen. Rachel told me of a slumber party, when she and her cousins were lying on the floor:

> *The gray house that sits on the same lot but more behind the big white house used to be the home of a doctor who committed suicide. One night I spent the night there with my younger cousin and my sister. We had made a big pallet in the dining room, which is between the kitchen and the living room. All three of us at once woke to someone stepping over and between us in the middle of the night, to find no one there. Then, a few weeks later* [my cousin's] *younger brother Tyler, who was two years old at the time, was sitting watching TV in the living room. He looked through the dining room towards the kitchen and started screaming and crying, saying the monster was coming towards him. He had to be taken out of the house and refused to go back inside. He described what seemed to be a man missing part of his face.*

Bayer Home, located on Aldine Westfield Road, after the road improvements that took both of the one-hundred-year-old oak trees from in front of the house. The old trees almost draped across the road, which many people said was spooky. *Author's collection.*

In the big white house, they would hear footsteps all the time that sounded like marching, or what they thought were the old rail workers going down the stairs to go to work, and it always happens around 4:00 a.m. Rachel said: "The big white house used to be a hotel back when the railroad was being built. There are still numbers hanging on some of the rooms upstairs. Every morning around 4:00 a.m., you can hear the men come down the stairs and go out the door to work on the railroad still."

The activity in the white house sounds like residual energy. It is the playback of the sound on the stairs, which is a sensory phenomenon, could be attributed to the routine event of going to work at the same time every day. It is similar to an echo or a replay of a past event. In this case, there's no attempted interaction between those living in the house and the spirits. There has not been found a way to stop residual hauntings. And we don't know the mechanism by which they are recorded in the first place. They can be very scary, but once people understand what's going on, most ignore it.

Wunsche Family Cemetery

I-45 Feeder Road
Spring, TX 77373

This is the family cemetery of one of the most notable families of Old Town Spring. The mid-1840s brought German immigrant Carl Wunsche from Saxony to Spring, Texas, which was established around 1838. Farmers would bring their cotton to Charles Wunsche's gin, which was located near town. Charles and Dell Wunsche built the Wunsche Brothers Saloon and Hotel in 1902 with leftover lumber from their own sawmill, which they had shut down. Their brother William Wunsche Sr., Ralph Hanks and Voress Bonin constructed the two-story building that still stands in Old Town Spring.

Part of the Wunsche family legacy includes Carl Wunsche Senior High School, which opened its doors in 2006. It was built on thirteen acres of land donated in 1937 by the family in the name of Carl Wunsche Sr. There have been several schools on this property, with the first being completed in 1939.

The cemetery is located in a small plot of land between the feeder road and the highway on the southeast side of I-45 and Cypresswood Drive. It features fewer than twenty graves, including Carl Wunsche Sr. and many of his descendants. Carl was born in Koengrich, Sachsen, Germany. He purchased the land that Wunsche Brothers Restaurant occupies.

The oldest marked grave in this cemetery is that of a five-year-old child: "M.O. Lorenz Wunsche." The youngest child buried there is the infant son

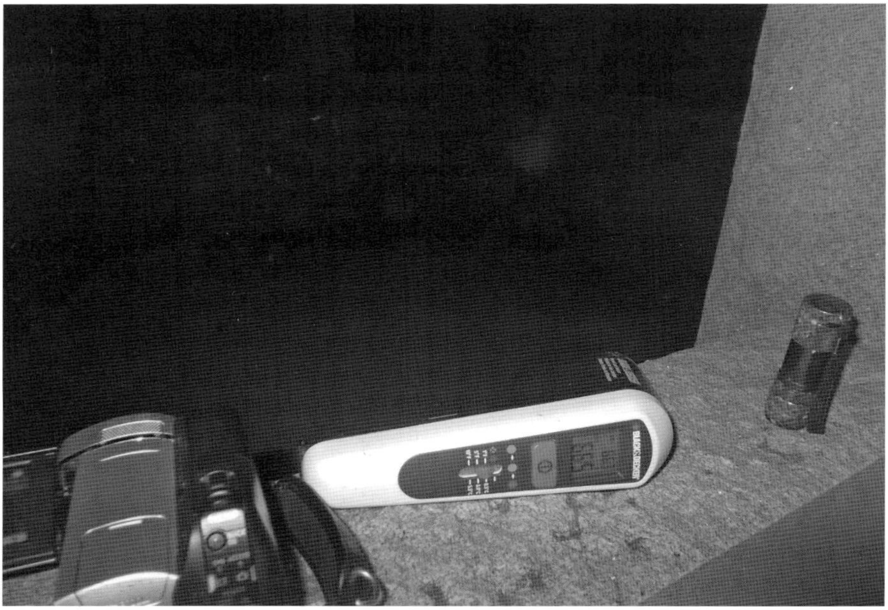

Some of the equipment we use for an investigation, including a TLD-100, which detects temperature changes when something passes in front of the beam. We also use video, audio recorders, flashlights and other essential equipment. *Author's collection.*

of Julia and Alvin Wunsche. He was born and died on August 9, 1941. Tombstone dates range from 1885 to 1959.

Olena Wunsche, born on July 6, 1908, is also buried at this site. The granddaughter of Carl Wunsche Sr., she was murdered along with her boyfriend while traveling back to Houston on May 6, 1929, at the age of twenty. When Olena was twenty years old, she worked as a cook during the week for a family in Houston. She was picked up on Fridays by her boyfriend, Edward Stone.

On the fateful weekend, Edward picked her up by driving down Highway 19, which is now I-45. They spent Saturday evening dancing at the Woodsman of the World Hall, which was located on the east side of Aldine Westfield between Spring School Road and Noble Street. Edward did not like to dance, but he enjoyed being there and watching others, including Olena, who danced to every song. The next day, Edward picked her up to drive her back to Houston. It was the last time the family saw them.

Investigators discovered that the couple had stopped in a bar by Aldine for a drink. They left and parked in an isolated spot—what was known as lovers' lane. Edward's body had been shot and was found outside the car. Olena's body was found in a different location along Aldine Westfield Road with shots to the back. They believed she jumped out and was gunned down. It is believed that they were ambushed and massacred. Some men and women were arrested, but it is believed that they were the wrong people, so they were released and never tried. In the mid-1950s, the case was reopened by Buster Kern, who later became a longtime sheriff of Harris County. He publicly announced that he had solved the murder, but nobody was named and no one was ever arrested or tried. To this day, the murder remains unsolved. You can visit the grave of Edward Stone in Budde Cemetery.

The cemetery has been investigated by many people because of its easy access. But its location right off the highway makes listening to audio difficult, due to the constant passing of cars. Several groups have uploaded photographs that appear to show possible apparitions. In one image, a shape that resembles a man is sitting on a headstone. It is said that you can see an old man with a white mustache and his nose and eyes. In another photo that looks like it was taken as part of a series in this area, there seems to be a woman's face with prominent cheekbones farther down from where this spirit man is.

I-45 DINER

19790 Interstate 45
Spring, TX 77373

Across the street from Spring High School is a strip center, and at one end is a diner. There have been several other restaurants in this location prior to the I-45 Diner. It stands on the former Wunsche homestead. The owners want you to know that this is the perfect place for delicious French toast, fluffy pancakes, juicy T-bones and the best Angus burgers. The food is cooked to perfection with the highest-quality ingredients. One of their slogans is, "Once you try us, you will surely want to come back for more."

Carl Wunsche and his family immigrated to Texas from Germany in 1846. Besides farming, the family had a gin and gristmill operation and eventually opened a sawmill. In the 1850s and '60s, the Wunsches had more than three thousand acres of land in the Spring area. The Wunsche Family Cemetery was a part of the homestead. The Wunsche Brothers are famous for building the Wunsche Brothers Saloon and Hotel in 1902. It stands in its original location near the tracks. The hotel was built to meet the growing needs of the railroad employees.

When Carl Wunsche came to Texas through Galveston, he didn't want to travel much farther. He came here with the dream of building a homestead where he could farm. The story is that he set off on foot with his oldest son. He went west in search for the best spot and, once he found it, was going to bring his family there. When he finally came upon Cypress Creek,

Woodlands Paranormal investigating one of many commercial locations we get asked to do each year. *Author's collection.*

it reminded him of their home in Germany. He bought a few acres to start, which was going for ten to twenty-five cents an acre. Over time, he purchased more property until he had amassed more than three thousand acres.

Old Montgomery Road would go on to become Highway 19; it was also called the Dallas Highway. It was first proposed in 1917 as one of the original twenty-six Texas state highways. The highway bisected the Spring area and ran through the original Wunsche homestead, which put the family cemetery beside a busy interstate. I was told the Wunsches were reluctant to sell the land to the state, agreeing only on the condition that the cemetery remain where it was.

At the diner, you can talk to the employees about the spirits that they believe are there. At night, they experience weird events. Among the interesting things that happen at the diner is that the employees hear their names being called. It happens all the time. When they ask around to see who needed something, no person says they did. Betty Pierce has worked at the diner for about a year now. She told me:

> *This place at about 10:30 takes on a new meaning. This was the actual homestead of the Wunsche family, and the graveyard sits right there. At*

night, we all get weird experiences. One night, somebody poked me in the back. There was a girl who was standing a good way away from me, and I asked her, "Did you just poke me in the back?" and she said "No." A few months later, Christian was mopping the floor and he felt somebody brush up against him like that, and it is just a weird feeling. All the hair on the back of your neck stands up. When I lock the doors, and leave here at night, I put my things by the door because I have to lock up. When I come down that dark hallway it's like something is right there right behind me. Sometimes you don't feel it, but when you do, its creepy. Then the other night, Carolyn and I were leaving. I was giving her a ride home and I had the lights off and was grabbing my purse and this light lit up in between us. I thought maybe a car did it, so I looked and there was nothing; looked in the kitchen and nobody was in the kitchen; and I looked at Carolyn and asked, "Did you see that?" and she said, "I'm out of here," and she took off running. I told her "Don't leave me in here," and she held the door open until I got there. It's just a very different feeling at night. When the owner was opening this place, somebody came in carrying something and she said that there was a dark shadow that ran behind the ice machine and she was very uncomfortable. It's just a really strange feeling that you get when you are here alone.

When Betty was first poked, she thought it was a kid. But then whatever is in the hallway, she says it is not little. The employees don't know what it is, but they don't like the uneasy feelings they get. Another staff member told me that she gets feelings at about 10:30 p.m.—it's just a weird thing that happens that she has a hard time explaining; the atmosphere somehow changes at that time.

PART III

UNDISCLOSED LOCATIONS

It's All Up in the Air

Spring, TX 77373

The Woodlands Paranormal team has been in and out of this interesting Old Spring home. We were called because the children were telling their mom that they were seeing things and were scared. They did not want to sleep in their rooms. The mom kept hearing weird things, noticed items moving around and saw things out of her peripheral vision.

We have caught very weird and unexplainable readings over the years. I have never seen this type of reading before, nor have I since. There was a line of EMF setting off the equipment. Think of EMF as an electrical current. It must have a beginning of sorts, a place where it is being generated that you can find. When we investigate, we pull out meters to get baseline readings from the environment before we start looking for anything. After the baseline, we spend hours looking for any anomaly, including EMF spikes. The theory is that spirits are made of energy, so we should be able to read that energy. We make notes of anything unusual. As an example, your refrigerator puts out a high reading; most plugs and appliances do as well, but that is normal.

While investigating one night at this location, we found an anomaly where the meters spiked and we were able to measure it out. It was three feet long by twelve inches wide and was six inches thick. It was about three feet off the floor, with no source for the electrical charge. Two feet above that was another line, similar but almost crossing the line below. Then, about two

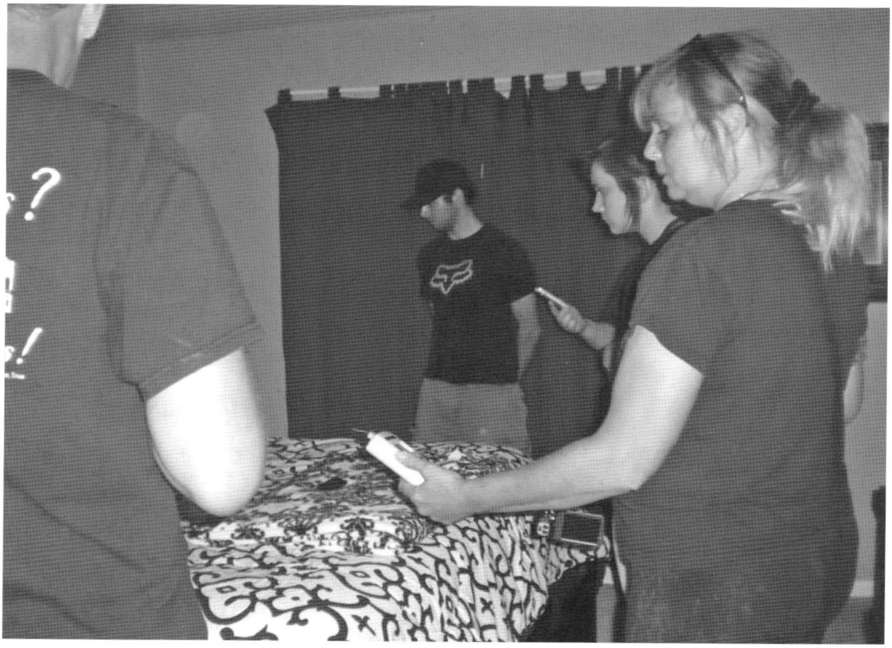

Above: Woodlands Paranormal investigating a Spring location where the family was very scared and needed help. *Author's collection.*

Left: This is one tool we use that helps us to visualize an apparition. It is a grid of green points of light that beam across a room. Anything that has density or can cause a shadow will break the beams, allowing us to see it moving through the room. *Author's collection.*

feet above that was a ball of EMF. This activity lingered for thirty minutes, during which time we were able to take all the measurements. The energy dissipated for about fifteen minutes and then came back again. This time, it had moved to a slightly different location in the same room.

We have also taken interesting photographs during our investigations here. We once heard a toilet lid slam down. A psychic medium believed that there was a spirit of a Native American who had lived before the area was settled. He was upset at the homeowners for being on his land. There is a cemetery near this location, in which the homeowners may experience transient spirits wandering through from time to time. But the dominant energy was from the spirit of this upset Native American. One of the homeowners worked in hospice and had a collection of things, including antiques from people who had passed away. Energy was picked up from some of these objects. Many hauntings are directly connected to objects.

THE SPRITE HOUSE

Spring, TX 77373

A homeowner contacted us to come out and investigate a case involving a baby. She told me about knocking and weird lights she kept seeing around her child. She was scared. She told me: "I live a life of paranormal things in my property and especially in the house around my children. I have lived in Spring for one year, and something is always happening around my one-year-old baby. There are lights that look like orbs that pass in front of the baby on the monitor all around my baby. I'm really scared [and] want to understand what this is. I'm not very good with English because I speak French but I still understand."

I went out the same day with another group member to do what we call an intake. She needed us to come to the house inconspicuously so as not to upset the neighbors. I assured her that we do not pull up with multiple vans and unload gobs of equipment with "ghost" labeled on everything. We also do not post anything that could identify her or the property unless she specifically approved of it.

We were in a hurry to get there because it was a case involving a baby. We went straight to the room where the baby was sleeping, took readings with our equipment and sat for a long time. We didn't observe anything unusual in the room. The homeowner wanted to show us her baby monitor. So, we left equipment running in the bedroom and began watching the baby from downstairs via the monitor.

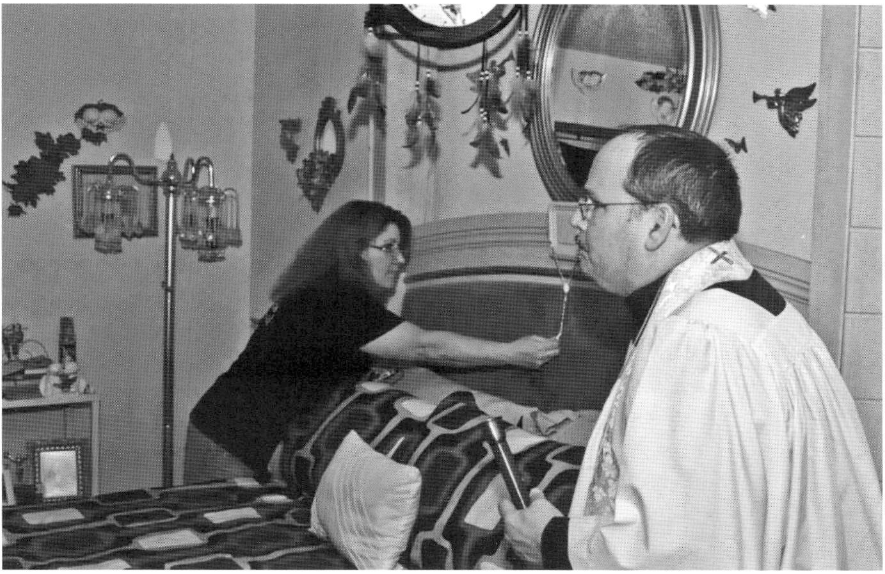

Woodlands Paranormal has several priests and pastors come out to help with cleansings. Here, Father Rob and I go through a Spring home. *Author's collection.*

Within thirty minutes of us being out of the room, we began to see on the monitor light anomalies come from out of nowhere and wrap around the baby. I have seen anomalies like this, but not going around a baby. We set up a time to come back that weekend with our whole group.

We arrived at the house that Saturday evening and set up our equipment with a special focus on the nursery. During our investigation, we captured EVP, photos, video and other anomalies all picked up with our equipment. The homeowner and the baby stayed for the investigation. At one point in the evening, she said that she felt like something cold was coming around her. We picked up a drop in temperature around her as well as EMF coming from around her arm, where she thought she was perhaps being touched. We took pictures of what we thought was a shadow. The photographs turned out clear, with a blurry streak running through it. I also took a photo of what appeared to be an entity moving behind one of our investigators. The video of some of our evidence from our investigation is on our YouTube channel. We have investigated her house multiple times. The mother said, "When my baby was five years old, he wasn't feeling well. He said he was seeing lots of things around him. I was with my husband. It was night, and he described a lot of dots of all kind of colors flying around him, and he said that he sees another person in the room."

We decided to call this the sprite house because of the light anomalies going on around the baby. (We were never able to scientifically explain them.) There was nothing negative going on in the home or around the baby. It was all just lights, feelings of coolness coming over the residents and the sensation of being watched. On another night, we investigated and brought a psychic medium with us onto the property to tell us what she sensed.

The psychic picked up on feelings of warmth and loving. She thought that, whatever the energy was, it seemed to be a woman. She believed the spirit was loving and thought that she had lost her own child. This woman had become attached to him and wanted to protect him. The mother was no longer afraid of whatever it was and thought that, maybe, it was even the baby's grandmother. We stayed in contact even after the family moved to Cypress. She still believes something good is hanging around her son and has never been scared since we left.

Right Around the Corner

Spring, TX 77373

We received an e-mail from the girlfriend of an owner of a Spring home who wishes to remain anonymous. He believed his house was haunted, and she wanted to help him. She wanted to be advised if there would be any charge for us to come and investigate the property. I responded to her e-mail, saying that we never charge to come out and investigate or help. Our correspondence went back and forth, with her explaining the things that were happening in his house.

> *I believe my boyfriend's house is haunted. It's mostly at night. He has been living there for more than 6 months now. He hears what sounds as if someone is trying to open his bedroom door. I heard it too when I was there to visit 2 weeks ago. He lives in Old Spring, TX. He thinks the previous owner practiced voodoo as when he first moved in for lots of reasons. I don't remember them all. He found spare change in every room and the "welcome" mat was facing inwards towards the house. He mostly feels like the sense of someone watching him from his room to the hallway towards the other rooms. It's a three-bedroom house. I'm not sure what additional information is needed to get to help him. He did mention he heard a lot of activity last night. Not sure if it can be investigated? Let me know please, thanks.*

One of the tools we use to investigate is video. Along with setting up a DVR system throughout the property, we use handheld cameras to get video. Here, Taylor films an investigation for an episode of *The Haunted*, which aired on Animal Planet. *Author's collection.*

I contacted the homeowner, who told me he had several doors that would make noise, as if someone was trying to break in. He found it upsetting because he was always getting up, ready to confront the people breaking into his house. He kept looking to see who was trying to get in and never found anyone. He thought perhaps he was going crazy, until his girlfriend heard it, too. He also complained that he heard noises in the attic that sounded like someone walking around. With all of these noises, he had a hard time sleeping and was always exhausted. He told me:

> *I have the feeling that something is there, and the electricity feeling is also always present. I heard the gate or the door knob turning, but definitely knocking, sometimes so hard that you can feel the wall vibrate. There is no specific time for this activity, now it just comes and goes at random.*

We arranged for a day to investigate the property. We set up our DVR system to catch activity at all the doors where he kept hearing sounds of a person trying to break in. We had someone that night sitting at the

This photo was taken in the Spring Historical Museum of the Victrola. Of two consecutively taken photographs, one was completely normal and in focus, but this one showed an anomaly. Both photos were taken with the same settings. *Author's collection.*

monitor watching the screen at all times to document anything. As we were investigating, we kept seeing shadows on the DVR system around the doors. We heard the sounds of a door knob jiggling and tapping. We tried to find out what was making the noises. One of our team felt pressure and tingling in his arm, like someone was trying to hold him.

While we were investigating, we were also filming a project for a production company in New York. We were in the garage, and I was interviewing Cathy Malis when we heard loud knocking coming from inside the garage but nobody was doing it. Throughout the night, there was other knocking and tapping noises. We ended our investigation with a cleansing of the home to see if that would help with the activity the homeowner was experiencing.

After we got home and reviewed everything, we found multiple photographs with anomalies. One was a light anomaly from inside the bedroom; there were several others, including one in the garage. We caught the loud knocking noise on video while we were filming. The homeowner wasn't scared anymore after we reviewed everything. Sage seemed to calm the activity down, so he was going to burn it if he was bothered by anything. He told me, "Wow! Interesting stuff going on here. It's cool that you captured this. Things have calmed down."

Possession or Depression

Spring, TX 77373

The following case was unusual for our team, because the call was from a mother who believed her baby was possessed. She told me that she had taken several photos that made her very scared. She said the water was always tuning on and off in the house for no reason, they saw shadows, felt like someone was looking at them, they were being touched and the baby always seemed to be looking at someone and screaming out of what she thought was fright. She had already sent the photos to a few other teams, but both were too far away to help. One team told her that they believed the photo showed a demon. They said that they ran the photo through some kind of software and thought it was proof that there was a demon around her baby and that she needed to get help from a priest.

I went out with half of my team that night and walked through the house to find out what had happened there. I sat with the homeowners to calm them down while my team tried to collect evidence. We scheduled a time for that weekend when we could put in some quality time with all of our equipment. We decided to get more help, so I invited several other paranormal teams that I trust. I called a psychic to do a walk-through the next day. She told me that she picked up on a grandfather.

During the investigation, Brian thought he saw something move into the wall. We also heard what sounded like whispering and dripping noises, but we could find no source. We debunked the photo of the light anomaly over

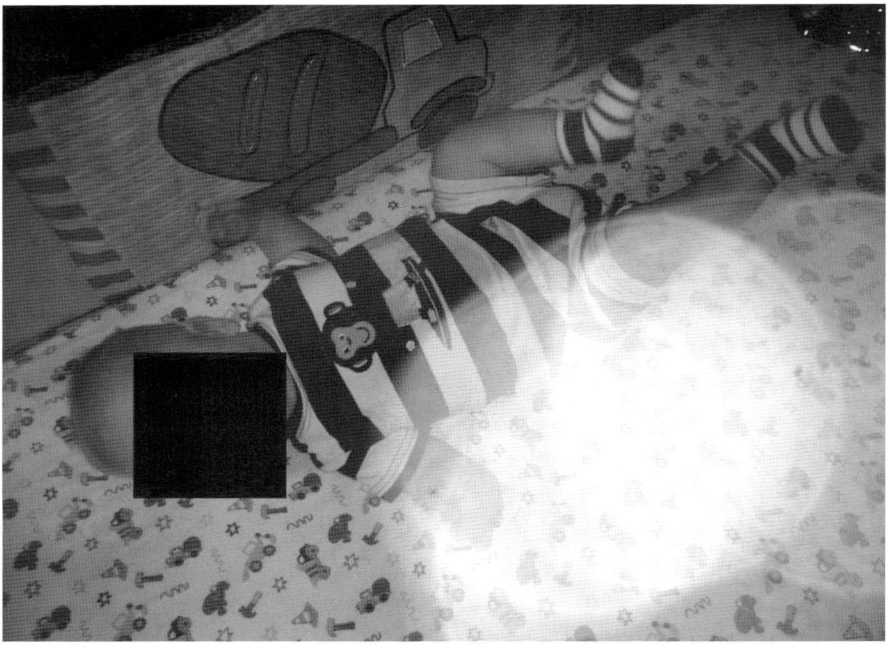

This anomaly was taken in Spring and submitted to several people who claimed it was demonic. During the investigation, I found a plastic turtle in the corner of the crib. It turned out to be the cause of the light anomaly you see here. In the top right corner of the photo can be seen light from the flash striking something reflective, which turned out to be the turtle. *Author's collection.*

the baby. Reflected light off of a toy turtle in his bed caused what looked like overlapping orbs. We did not find anything negative in the house and wanted the mom to calm down. I talked to her husband for a while. He told me that she had got almost no sleep since the baby was born. I told him that I thought that she could be suffering from postpartum depression and psychosis. She needed to go to her doctor for help and to get sleep.

We caught multiple EVPs in the investigation. In one EVP, I can be heard telling everyone that I wanted to talk in a normal voice. Christian said "Ok," and within ten seconds we caught a voice saying "Please." This would indicate that whatever was there is intelligent. We caught dripping noises. Brian thought he saw something move into the wall, and we caught a voice saying "Yea." I caught a voice that said "The man" when we were sitting on the balcony, and I kept hearing whispering and knocking noises. I sent the information to the woman's husband. He told me she had gone to her doctor.

Father Robert Hall, Kenneth Melton and Jordan Nance with Woodlands Paranormal conducting a house cleansing. *Author's collection.*

One of the serious, yet fun, tools we use in investigations is called the TLD-100. It measures temperature changes from one to ten degrees, indicated by changes in color. If the temperature drops, the green light changes to blue; if the temperature increases, the light changes to red. *Author's collection.*

Their house seemed to have activity, but none of it was what we would consider negative. The mom was most likely misjudging the baby's screams, thinking something was there when the baby was just hungry. The baby was also showing signs of being colicky. The baby could have also seen something, but we will never know. We were afraid that since the mother had just delivered the baby, she might be taking normal noises that go on in a house as those of a demon. We also thought she was hallucinating.

BIBLIOGRAPHY

Books and Periodicals

Abbott, Olyve Hallmark. *Texas Ghosts: Galveston, Houston, and Vicinity*. Atglen, PA: Schiffer Publishing, Ltd., 2010.

American Association of University Women. *The Heritage of North Harris County*. Harris County Public Library, April 1986. Accessed January 2017. texashistory.unt.edu/ark:/67531/metapth611550.

Gilbert, Kasey. *The Ghosts of Old Town Spring: History and Hauntings of North Harris County Texas*. N.p.: Boothill Press, 2013.

Houston Post 33, no. 247 (December 7, 1917).

Journal of the Society for Psychical Research 62, no. 851 (April 1998).

North Harris County News 1, no. 1 (August 9, 1967).

Old Town Spring Souvenir Newspaper.

Schensul, Jill. "If You Go to Key West, Fla., Beware of Robert the Doll." *North Jersey News*, March 28, 2017.

Smith, Margaret Mallott. *Spring Through the Seasons: Stories of a Texas Town*. Fort Worth, TX: Sunbelt-Eakin, 2001.

Stack, Megan K. "Houston-Area Woman Says Her Job Is Really All a Matter of Heart." *Dallas Morning News*, n.d.

Texas Historical Commission. "Historic Marker Application: Wunsche Bros. Saloon and Hotel." June 7, 1984.

United States Geological Survey. *Spring Quadrangle* (map). Reston, VA: 1920.

Williams, Scott. *Haunted Texas: A Travel Guide*. Guilford, CT: Globe Pequot, 2007.

Young, Samuel Oliver. *True Stories of Old Houston and Houstonians: Historical and Personal Sketches*. Galveston, TX, 1913.

Internet Sources

Brookwood Community. http://www.brookwoodcommunity.org/blog/book-release-everybodys-got-a-seed-to-sow-the-brookwood-story.

Chicago Tribune. http://articles.chicagotribune.com/2013-06-19/news/ct-x-dying-words-0619-20130619_1_hospice-nurse-maggie-callanan-death-awareness.

Genealogy Trails. http://www.genealogytrails.com/tex/state/legalhangings.html.

Handbook of Texas Online. https://tshaonline.org/handbook/online/articles/hls74.

Harris County Commissioner Precinct 4. http://www.hcp4.net/Community/HistoricalMarkers/Spring.

Houston Architecture. http://www.houstonarchitecture.com/haif/topic/18415-history-of-schools-in-aldine-isd.

Houston Chronicle. http://www.chron.com/neighborhood/cyfair-news/article/Old-Town-Spring-tour-casts-light-on-haunted-2115644.php.

Old Corky. http://oldcorky.com/May09.pdf.

Old Town Spring. http://oldtownspring.com/info/history.

On the Tudor Trail. http://onthetudortrail.com/Blog/anne-boleyn/ghost-of-anne-boleyn-the-stories.

Out About Texas. http://www.outabouttexas.com/LocSrv?locId=5490320045244416.

Royal Museums Greenwich. http://www.rmg.co.uk/see-do/we-recommend/attractions/great-hall-tulip-stairs.

South Writ Large. http://southwritlarge.com/articles/the-curse-of-old-town-spring.

Texas History. https://texashistory.unt.edu/ark:/67531/metapth455835/?q=spring.

Texas State Historical Association. http://www.tshaonline.org/handbook/online/articles/jgl01.

Time. http://content.time.com/time/magazine/article/0,9171,907718-1,00.html.

Yorkshire Ghost. http://www.yorkshireghosts.co.uk.

About the Author

Cathy Nance is the founder and case manager of Woodlands Paranormal. As an intuitive and empath, Cathy has been on a lifelong journey for helping others, as well as exploring and learning about everything she had an interest in. She has used her gifts as the case manager of OKPRI, Society of the Haunted and then Woodlands Paranormal, where she counsels the group's clients and manages the group.

After several near-death experiences at the age of three, she began to have strange things happen that nobody could explain. She would dismiss anything strange, because she thought she was tired, or she would rationalize it to fit the most logical explanation. Cathy grew up in the church and found some explanations through priests and her religious studies. She says, "As I got older, I moved into a very old home with paranormal activity and couldn't always explain it away. I started seeking more answers by reading everything I could get my hands on as well as asking questions from anyone who would talk about it. I took some classes in parapsychology and became even more devout in my church and spirituality."

Her work in the paranormal has led her to be featured on Animal Planet's television show *The Haunted* (seasons 1 and 2) as well as *My Ghost Story* on the Biography Channel, *Ghosts and Legends of Oklahoma* on GTN Television Network and multiple film projects.

About the Author

Apart from her paranormal interests, Cathy is the owner and photographer of Cathy Nance Studios, located in Old Town Spring, Texas. Photography is one of the mediums that she uses to create art for her clients. She has had her art and photography on display in various galleries. She is also a nurse and an accomplished pastry chef.

Visit us at
www.historypress.net

This title is also available as an e-book